Call Out the Cadets

THE BATTLE OF NEW MARKET
MAY 15, 1864

by Sarah Kay Bierle

EMERGING CIVIL WAR SERIES

Chris Mackowski, series editor
Chris Kolakowski, chief historian

The Emerging Civil War Series

offers compelling, easy-to-read overviews of some of the Civil War's most important battles and stories.

Recipient of the Army Historical Foundation's Lieutenant General Richard G. Trefry Award for contributions to the literature on the history of the U.S. Army

Also part of the Emerging Civil War Series:

For a complete list of titles in the Emerging Civil War Series, visit www.emergingcivilwar.com.

Call Out the Cadets

THE BATTLE OF NEW MARKET
MAY 15, 1864

by Sarah Kay Bierle

EMERGING CIVIL WAR SERIES

SB
Savas Beatie
California

First edition, first printing

ISBN-13 (paperback): 978-1-61121-469-7
ISBN-13 (ebook): 978-1-61121-470-3

Library of Congress Cataloging-in-Publication Data

Names: Bierle, Sarah Kay, author.
Title: Call out the cadets : the Battle of New Market, May 15, 1864 / by Sarah Kay Bierle.
Other titles: Battle of New Market, May 15, 1864
Description: El Dorado Hills, California : Savas Beatie, [2019] |
Series: Emerging civil war series | Includes bibliographical references.
Identifiers: LCCN 2019008418| ISBN 9781611214697 (pbk : alk. paper) |
ISBN 9781611214703 (ebk)
Subjects: LCSH: New Market, Battle of, New Market, Va., 1864. |
Virginia--History--Civil War, 1861-1865. | Military
cadets--Virginia--History--19th century. | Virginia Military
Institute--History--19th century. | Soldiers--Virginia--History--19th
century. | Soldiers--Confederate States of America--History--19th century.
| United States--History--Civil War, 1861-1865.
Classification: LCC E476.64 .B54 2019 | DDC 975.5/03--dc23
LC record available at https://lccn.loc.gov/2019008418

SB

Published by
Savas Beatie LLC
989 Governor Drive, Suite 102
El Dorado Hills, California 95762
Phone: 916-941-6896
Email: sales@savasbeatie.com
Web: www.savasbeatie.com

Savas Beatie titles are available at special discounts for bulk purchases in the United States by corporations, institutions, and other organizations. For more details, please contact Special Sales, 989 Governor Drive, Ste 102, El Dorado Hills, CA 95762, or you may e-mail us at sales@savasbeatie.com, or visit our website at www.savasbeatie.com for additional information.

To my brothers—Josiah and Nathan—
young men who desire to serve with honor.

"All things are ready if our minds be so."
—Shakespeare's *Henry V*

Table of Contents

Footnotes for this volume are available at
http://emergingcivilwar.com/publications/the-emerging-civil-war-series/footnotes

* * *

List of Maps

Maps by Hal Jespersen

Acknowledgments

Armies do not suddenly and without reason materialize on a battlefield, and a book does not suddenly spring into being. The journey to place this book in your hands has been a proverbial road as rough and smooth as the Old Valley Pike that originally brought the armies to New Market. I'm grateful to all who have been part of this journey:

Through their house and basement windows, the Bushong family witnessed the arrival of the armies and the battle that would change their town and family history. Earlier in the year, they would have seen a quieter, placid scene like this one. (skb)

Chris Mackowski, editor-in-chief at Emerging Civil War, convinced me to write a book for the ECW series and has helped me become a better, braver writer.

Colonel Keith Gibson, Executive Director of the Virginia Military Institute Museum System, has welcomed this new book and taken time to give advice and prepare the foreword.

Colonel Diane Jacobs and Ms. Mary Laura Kludy graciously let me spend days in the Virginia Military Institute Archive, reading (or photographing) stacks of primary sources.

Lt. Colonel Troy Marshall considerately shared resources, discussion time, battlefield tips, and sites to visit during my trips to New Market, challenging me to write a book that will draw a reader to the history and leave them wanting to know even more.

Dan Davis, my colleague from ECW, kindly came to New Market to teach this California girl how to "read a battlefield"…in a rainstorm.

Dara Green, Keven Walker, and the staff at Shenandoah Valley Battlefields Foundation have anticipated this book and assisted with local details and shared information about new preservation efforts on or near the battlefield.

Hal Jespersen meticulously prepared the campaign and battle maps for this book, sharing his expertise and cartography skills.

The librarians, archivists, and staff at The Huntington Library in San Marino, California, and the Lincoln Memorial Shrine Archive assisted by retrieving amazing resources and helping a new researcher feel welcomed to this brave new world of silent rooms and treasured sources.

Mike Breckenridge and Bruce A. Smith, living history enthusiasts, took time from their busy schedules to discuss the battle of New Market, Hart's Engineers, and Union cavalry. They have anxiously asked about the book nearly every time we've met!

Susan C. Bierle, my mom, agreed to be my first reader and point out the areas of the manuscript that needed more detail or clarification.

Many thanks to the publishing team at Savas Beatie for their untiring belief in this book, for its amazing cover, and for the professional skills to turn a manuscript into a real volume, a dream into reality.

Accounts from soldiers at New Market mention a waterway at the bottom of the hollow between Shirley's Hill and Manor's Hill—yet another obstacle for the advancing Confederates. Somewhere in the hollow, the cadets left much of their march gear; unfortunately, when they returned for their possessions at the end of the fight, they discovered that they had been stolen. (skb)

PHOTO CREDITS: Sarah Kay Bierle (skb), Find a Grave (fag); Library of Congress (loc); Charles H. Lynch, *The Civil War Diary, 1862-1865, of Charles H. Lynch 18th Conn. Vol's* (cl); National Park Service (nps); New Market Historical Society (nmhs); Virginia Military Institute Archives (vmi); Wikipedia Commons (wc)

For the Emerging Civil War Series

Theodore P. Savas, *publisher*
Chris Mackowski, *series editor*
Christopher Kolakowski, *chief historian*
Sarah Keeney, *editorial consultant*
Kristopher D. White, *co-founding editor*

Maps by Hal Jespersen
Design and layout by Chris Mackowski

Touring the Battlefield

The tour notes provided in this book incorporate sites featured in New Market State Battlefield State Historical Park and the Shenandoah Valley Battlefields Foundation's tours of the area, along with a few locations off the beaten path. Several of the sites are located within New Market Battlefield State Historical Park, and these are accessible with a purchased visitor pass.

I-81 runs straight through the middle of the New Market battlefield, providing some challenges for hiking, touring, and topographical study. However, most of the key positions and landmarks from the battle have been preserved; it just takes a little imagination to see the landscape without the rushing trucks and cars. Route 11 follows the Old Valley Pike, a well-established road in 1864, and several of the tour stops are along this highway.

From New Market, the modern road follows the Old Valley Pike over Rude's Hill on the northward journey back to the Shenandoah River crossing at Mount Jackson. Union troops hurried along this route after their lines collapsed during the battle. (skb)

A few safety tips around New Market: Please note there are not safe pull-outs on the drive along Route 211 to the top of New Market Gap to view the scenery; use extra caution when exiting the trailhead parking lot at the top of the mountain. Along Route 11, the historic interpretative signs and pull outs are on the west side of the road; the tour notes purposely instruct explorers to drive north, then visit the sites when returning south.

Safe travels and special exploring moments!

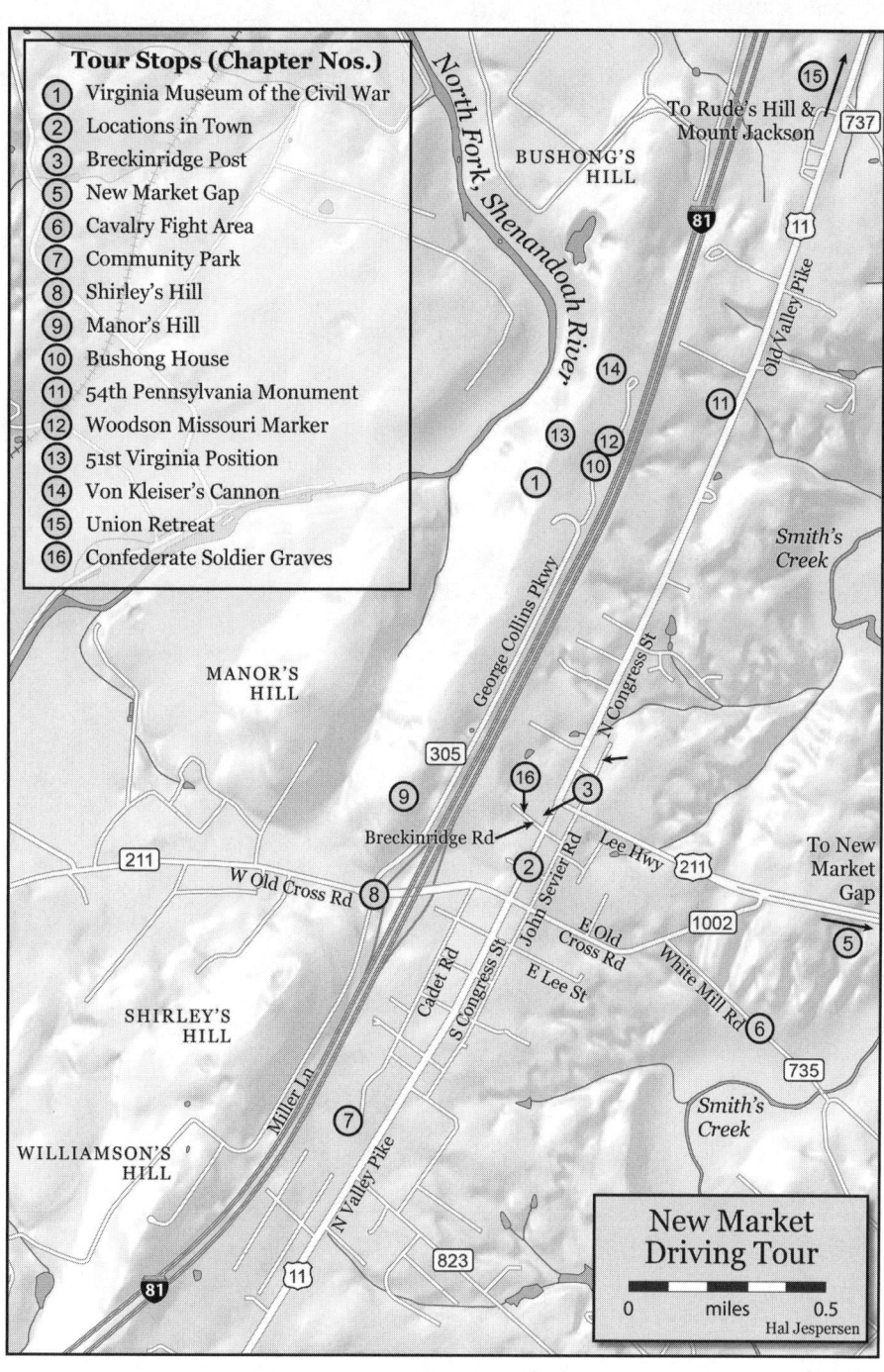

Tour Stops (Chapter Nos.)

1. Virginia Museum of the Civil War
2. Locations in Town
3. Breckinridge Post
5. New Market Gap
6. Cavalry Fight Area
7. Community Park
8. Shirley's Hill
9. Manor's Hill
10. Bushong House
11. 54th Pennsylvania Monument
12. Woodson Missouri Marker
13. 51st Virginia Position
14. Von Kleiser's Cannon
15. Union Retreat
16. Confederate Soldier Graves

New Market Driving Tour

0   miles   0.5

Hal Jespersen

NEW MARKET DRIVING TOUR—This map shows the tour stops on the ECW driving tour. Please note that Stop 4 is the Virginia Military Institute in Lexington, Virginia, not pictured on this map. Safe travels and best wishes for memorable explorations.

This cannon stands guard over the "Field of Lost Shoes"—representing the Union gun captured by the VMI Cadets and a reminder of the stories of courage on both sides of the field. (skb)

Foreword

BY COL. KEITH E. GIBSON

This story has been told many times. Why again?

The battle of New Market is perhaps the most written about secondary battle of the American Civil War. There is good reason for the attention it has been given: it is the only time in American history in which a college student body—the Virginia Military Institute Cadet Corps—participated in pitched battle as an independent unit. When the fight was over, the commanding general singled out the cadets for achieving a hard fought victory.

This is the story now told by Sarah Kay Bierle in a fresh and engaging way. Relying on the words of those who were there, she weaves a compelling narrative of duty, commitment, and courage. But she does more than tell the story; Ms. Bierle challenges us to reflect on the life-changing, transformative experiences of this battle for those who were there. She indentifies a very specific spot—a split rail fence, or dirt lane, or farm house—a spot where you can stand today, and which places you there in the firing line, or on the march, or in the makeshift hospital. The author accomplishes all of this is in a fast-paced, immensely readable style.

Ms. Bierle also provides a comprehensive driving tour. There is no better way to understand the events of May 15, 1864—or of any historical event, really—than to stand on the ground where the event took place. Together, the narrative and the tour provide a complete and rewarding experience.

It is a story worth retelling.

COLONEL KEITH E. GIBSON *is the director of the Virginia Military Institute Museum System.*

"We are decimated!
It is madness to pause here!
We must charge or fly.
And *charge* it was...."

— *John S. Wise*

"They Will Fight"

PROLOGUE

"General, why don't you put the cadets in line? They will fight as well as our men," insisted Maj. Charles Semple as the officers peered through the battle smoke and rain. Confederate regiments on the battle line had separated, leaving a gap in the infantry position along the split rail fence, which the active Union officers would likely exploit if the hole was not filled soon.

Major General John C. Breckinridge waited, agonizing over the decision to launch the cadets from the Virginia Military Institute into the intense fire. "No, Charley, this will not do," he finally said. "They are only children and I cannot expose them to such a fire as our center will receive." Semple rode off through the mud and attempted to shift the troops already engaged to fill the gap. Finding it impossible, he returned. Whether the general liked it or not, it was time to send in the cadets— to use them for the very purpose they had been called out to accomplish.

Just five days earlier, the boys from VMI had been tending to their ceremonial and academic duties at their barracks school nearly eighty miles south of the thunder-filled field at New Market. The cadets—ranging in age from fifteen to twenty-five—had dreamed of escaping school and fighting in the real war. Confederate General Breckinridge had reluctantly issued the orders, calling the boys from their school and instructing them to join his reduced army before the battle that might decide the fate of the Shenandoah Valley. They had arrived with the rest of Breckinridge's hastily assembled army, marching throughout the previous night to reach New Market.

The replica rail fence on New Market Battlefield marking the location of the cadets' position on the Confederate battle line. (skb)

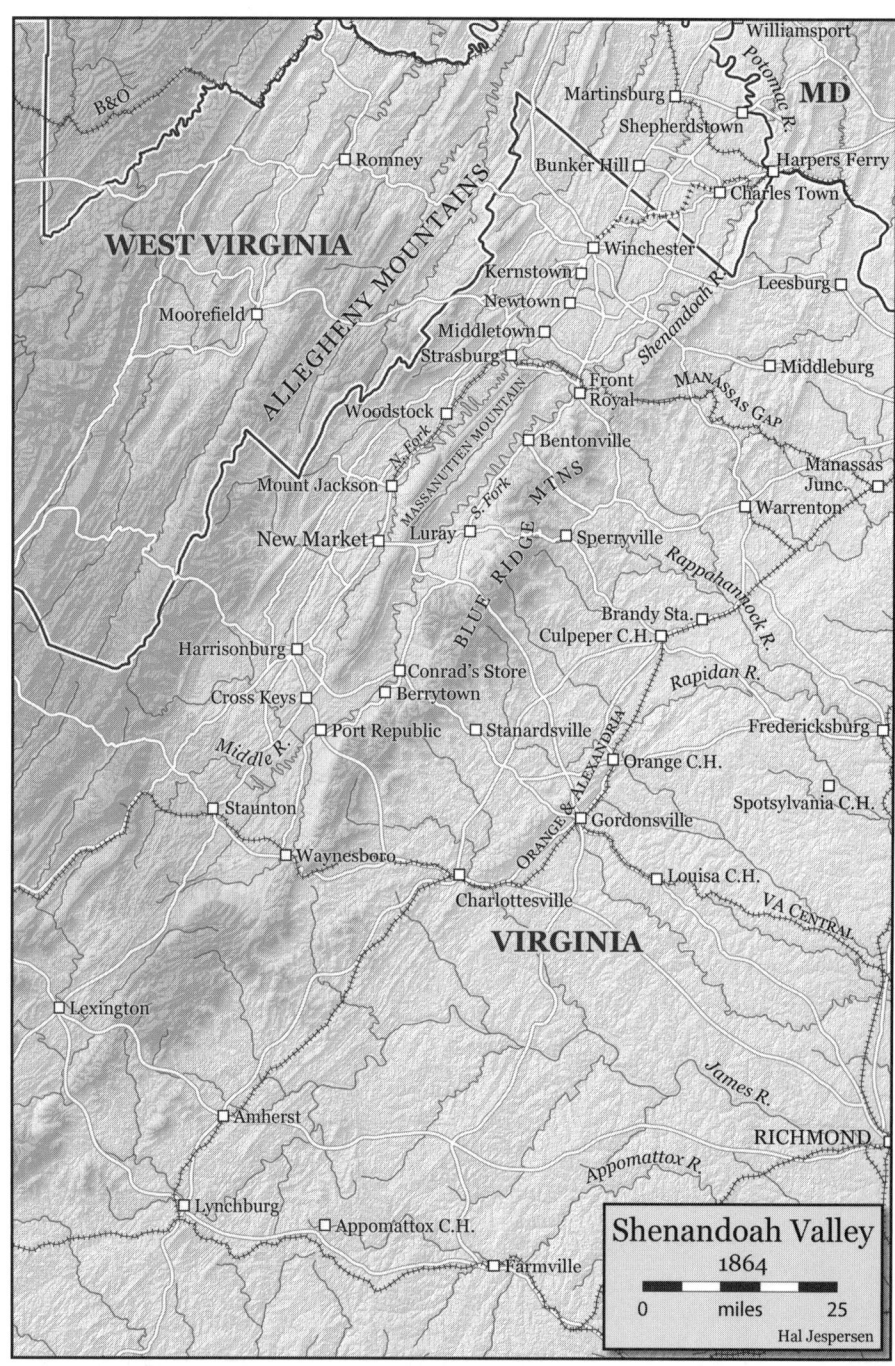

SHENANDOAH VALLEY—The Shenandoah Valley had already been fought over for years. The ridges, rivers, roads, and bridges all played a part in a mighty contest for domination and rebellion in this fertile agricultural region. Keep in mind that, due to the elevations and course of the Shenandoah River, moving "up the Valley" means moving South and "down the Valley" indicates moving North.

For most of the morning's fight, Breckinridge had kept the cadets in reserve and out of direct fire. They had taken hits on their march down Shirley's Hill, awakening to the realization that war's tragedies muted its glories. Now, with a desperate situation unfolding on his battle line, Breckinridge gave in. The boys were a trained military force, untried in battle but filled with enthusiasm and a deep commitment to comradeship and honor that might hold them steady in the vortex of battle.

Moments later, the four companies of cadets ploughed across an open field, split around the Bushong farm buildings, scrambled through the orchard, and reached the battle position at the split rail fence. To their left in this battle position, two Virginia regiments blazed away at the Federals on Bushong's Hill while to the right remnant units stubbornly clung to their line, taking massive casualties. Across an open, flooded field, Union soldiers—some of them also in their teens—stood their ground without shelter, charging forward and falling back to defensive positions as the tide of battle ebbed and flowed with its ever costly toll. A Union battery plied its deadly work directly in front of the cadets while other artillery created a devastating crossfire.

On a clear day, it is easy to see across the "Field of Lost Shoes," but during the battle, this view was heavily obscured by smoke and rain. (skb)

The cadets formed at the simple rail fence that separated the orchard and north field on Jacob Bushong's farm. Here, they stood, crouched, or lay. They fired back at the Yankees, tended to injured comrades, and found a whole new vocabulary to vent their battle fears.

At a certain moment, that rail fence—a line guide, an imaginary shelter—transformed to a threshold: a boundary between victory and defeat, courage and cowardice, boyhood and manhood. At a certain moment, the boys who had been called from their studies, whose families believed they were safe from battle, rose up. They knew the dangers of standing in battle fire and the dangers of open fields. But they rose up, and Breckinridge's battle—and their own lives—would be irrevocably altered. They would never be ordinary again.

John B. Gray, one of the VMI Cadets who fought at New Market, was seventeen in mid-May 1864; like his comrades, he made the decision to go forward at a decisive moment in the fight. (vmi)

Before the Battle Came

CHAPTER ONE

MAY 1864

At the beginning of May 1864, Jacob Bushong could stand on his porch and look with satisfaction on his farm property. The newly-planted fields stretched away from the house, large barn, and outbuildings. The orchard, to the north, offered promise of a good harvest of apples, cherries, pears, and quince later in the year. He had built a good life with his wife, Sarah Strickler Bushong, and raised three surviving children on his farm, located north and west of the small crossroads town of New Market. His farm had prospered through the years, and he regularly interacted and conducted business with his neighbors in the community.

If he looked east, Mr. Bushong could see New Market Gap in Massanutten Mountain, which transected the northern central part of the Shenandoah Valley and created the Luray Valley beyond. Bordering his property on the west, the Shenandoah River flowed beneath high bluffs on its south-to-north journey, running down Virginia's great valley to empty into the Potomac River at Harper's Ferry, some eighty miles to the north.

A dirt lane connected his farm to the Valley Turnpike, the great commercial highway networking the large towns and small villages of the Shenandoah Valley. Originally built along a north-south trail used by Native American hunters and warriors and part of the Great Wagon Road utilized by colonial settlers, the macadamized turnpike's construction began in 1834. By the mid-19th Century, the supply wagons, stagecoaches, travelers, and locals used the highway extensively, paying tolls along the way. When

The Bushong House—an original structure that stood during the battle—has been carefully restored by the staff and volunteers at New Market Battlefield State Historical Park and is now used to emphasize the civilian side of the battle history. (skb)

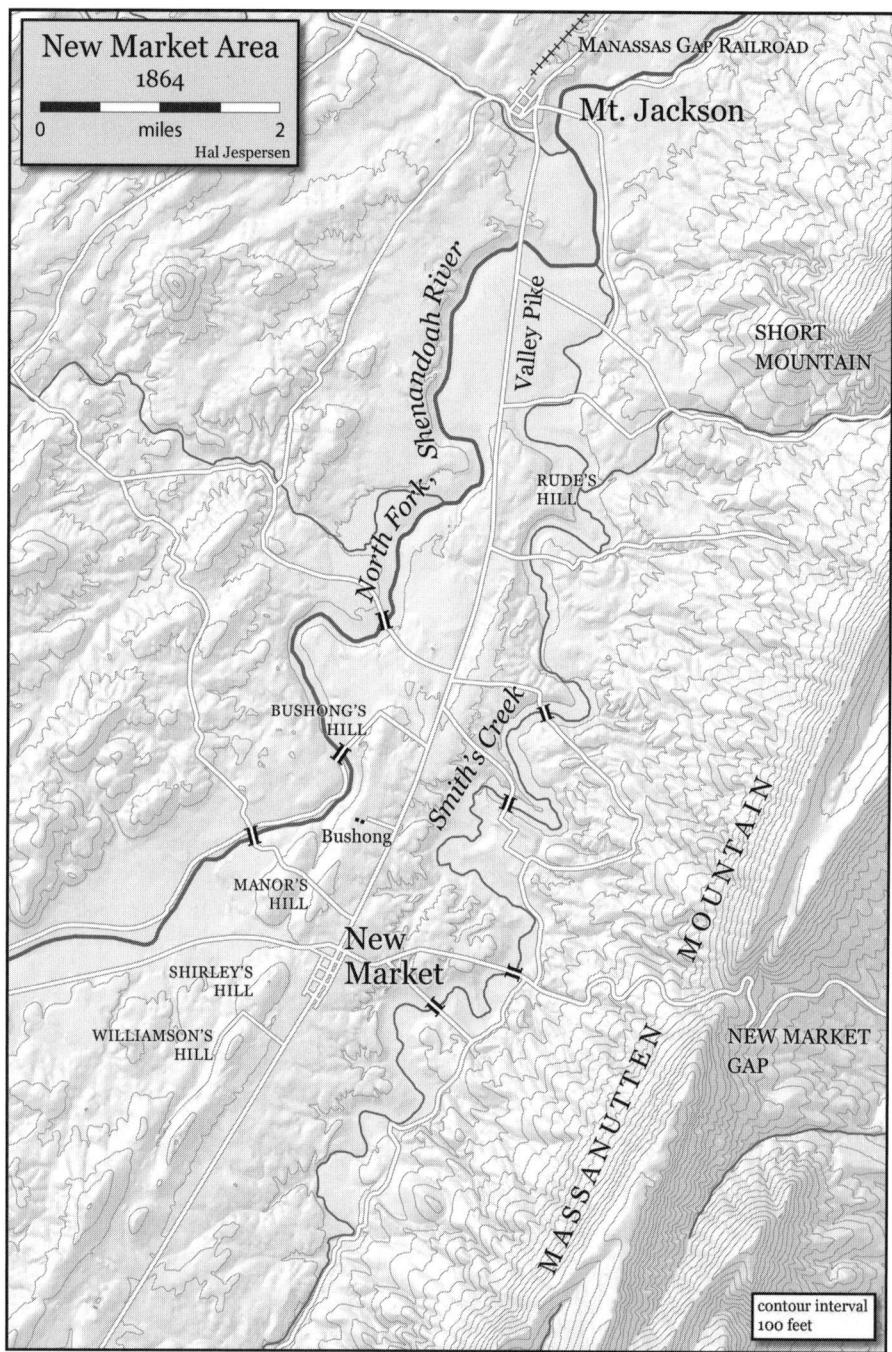

New Market Area
1864
0   miles   2
Hal Jespersen

MANASSAS GAP RAILROAD

Mt. Jackson

SHORT MOUNTAIN

North Fork, Shenandoah River

Valley Pike

RUDE'S HILL

BUSHONG'S HILL

Smith's Creek

Bushong

MANOR'S HILL

New Market

SHIRLEY'S HILL

WILLIAMSON'S HILL

MASSANUTTEN MOUNTAIN

NEW MARKET GAP

contour interval
100 feet

NEW MARKET AREA—A crossroads town, New Market sits between the Shenandoah River and Smith Creek with several hills rising immediately southwest and northwest of the village.

the Civil War began in 1861, officers quickly learned that this "avenue for armies" allowed them to conveniently and swiftly move troops through the Shenandoah Valley. The Valley—known for its agricultural production—created a tempting prize for Union armies and a treasure to preserve for the Confederacy. Along with its agricultural significance, the valley between

This historic image of the Bushongs' barn (post-Civil War) illustrates the importance of shelter for animals and harvested crops in agricultural communities. (vmi)

the Blue Ridge and Allegheny mountains offered strategic advantage, allowing opportunities to threaten Washington City or Richmond by a back-door approach.

One of the earliest defenders of the Shenandoah Valley—General Thomas J. "Stonewall" Jackson—recognized its importance, writing, "If the Valley is lost, Virginia is lost." In the spring of 1862, Jackson and his weary army marched past the Bushong farm and through New Market village several times as they strode hundreds of miles, fought six battles, and defeated three Union armies in approximately seven weeks. Later that year, Jackson briefly made his headquarters at the Strayer House in town, and Union troops had made their share of appearances in the community.

Situated in the heart of Virginia's Shenandoah Valley, the small town of New Market had seen armies come and go along the turnpike. The crossroads location had witnessed warring parties for centuries as Native American tribes used the north-south track and a trail running west to east from Brock Gap in the Alleghenies to New Market Gap through Luray Valley to Thornton Gap in the Blue Ridge Mountains for peaceful or warring journeys. Colonial settler John Sevier is usually credited for establishing New Market, though he resided there only a short time. Named for New Market, England, the fledging colonial village boasted a racetrack, like its English predecessor. In 1796, an act of the General Assembly of Virginia officially established the town, which grew and prospered in the next decades.

According to the Gazetteer of Virginia in 1835, New Market was

three-fourth of a mile in length, containing above one hundred dwelling houses, with a population of 700 persons. The streets are remarkably level, straight and well laid out... nearly parallel with the Massanutten mountain and two miles distant from its base. There are 3 houses of public worship, viz. 1 Lutheran, 1 Baptist, and 1 Methodist, 1 large and commodious brick academy in which is taught all the branches

This quilt, made by Miss Elizabeth A. Bushong in the 1850's, is carefully preserved and displayed by Virginia Museum of the Civil War. (skb)

of liberal and polite education, 1 book and job printing office, 5 stores, 3 taverns, 1 resident attorney, and 4 regular physicians. There is perhaps no town in the state of the same size, where the mechanical pursuits are carried on to a greater extent than in this. There are here in active and extensive operation 1 manufactory of threshing machines, 2 wheelwrights, 4 cabinet makers and house-joiners, 4 tanneries, 2 saddle and harness making establishments, 2 chair factories, 4 boot and shoe manufactories, 3 hat factories, 1 silversmith and jeweler, 1 coppersmith and tin plate worker, 2 gunsmiths, 2 blacksmiths, 1 locksmith, 1 sleymaker, 1 saddle-tree maker, 1 diaper weaver, and 2 potteries, at one of which stoneware of superior quality is manufactured. There are also in the vicinity 2 forges for the manufactory of pig metal into bar iron, both of which are at this time in active operation. The country around abounds in iron ore of the best quality.

The town's prosperity continued through the next decades, and by 1860, on the eve of the Civil War, 1,422 people called New Market "home;" among those residents, fifty-five free blacks, and seventy-nine slaves lived in the same community with 1,288 whites.

The voting citizens of New Market and Shenandoah Country generally supported John Breckinridge in the 1860 presidential election and more openly supported or accepted secession than other Valley residents. Jacob Bushong and his neighbors hardly imagined that less than four years

after that election, their preferred candidate would direct a battle in their streets and fields.

New Market had its own militia unit, which had witnessed John Brown's trial and death. Known as the Tenth Legion Artillery though it was an artillery unit in name only, this unit responded to Governor Wise's call and stood guard duty for the radical abolitionist and his conspirators' trial and execution in 1859. Franklin Bushong—one of Jacob's and Sarah's sons—served in this militia unit and witnessed the hangings. Also in 1859, the New Market Cavalry formed under command of Capt. W. H. Rice. When the Civil War began, the New Market Cavalry enthusiastically joined the Confederate forces, becoming Rice's Battery and serving in important campaigns and battles.

Though the community had experienced war and seen encampments and marching soldiers, it had thus far escaped Union occupation or even major interaction with Yankees, unlike the towns farther down the Valley. New Market's turn to see war first-hand would come, though.

In the spring of 1864—while Grant's Union forces and Lee's Confederate troops maneuvered, struck, and defended through the Overland Campaign beyond the Blue Ridge Mountains—New Market citizens trembled as the newest Yankee invasion of the Shenandoah Valley brought columns of troops closer to their quiet community. Jacob Bushong, his neighbors on nearby farms, and his acquaintances in town would soon find

New Market Gap as it appears from near where the Bushong's farm lane joined the Old Valley Turnpike. Unfortunately, the modern interstate highway blocks the wonderful, clear view the family must have enjoyed of the gap during the 19th Century. (skb)

themselves in the midst of military combat. The experiences of that year would be far from what one might anticipate gazing over newly planted fields and gardens.

In New Market

Virginia Museum of the Civil War is located at the heart of New Market Battlefield. This part of the museum's architecture was designed to look like a drum with stacked rifles; much of the exterior and interior features of the building are symbolic of the history and legacy of courage at New Market. (skb)

Follow the "brown signs" like this one to the Virginia Museum of the Civil War and New Market Battlefield State Historical Park. Located along the interstate highway and around town, these signs are excellent guideposts. (skb)

Begin the tour at the Virginia Museum of the Civil War on New Market Battlefield. If you are traveling on Interstate Route 81, exit at Old Cross Road (exit 264) and follow the brown signs to the museum on George R. Collins Memorial Parkway. Be sure to drive all the way to the end of the road to find the Virginia Museum of the Civil War, which is a large, drum-shaped building.

The Virginia Museum of the Civil War at New Market Battlefield State Historical Park offers wonderful displays and a historic documentary relating to the local battle and the state's role in the 1860s conflict. You may want to take time to explore the museum now or return later in the tour, which will come back to this point as you move through the battle chronologically. Please note the closing times for the museum and state historic park. If you will not have time to come back during the Emerging Civil War tour, we recommend touring the museum and hiking this portion of the battlefield now, using the tour notes beginning in Chapter 9.

Ready to head into the town of New Market?

Exit the museum parking lot, following the exit signs and arrows. As you exit the gate, you'll be on George R. Collins Memorial Parkway (Road 305). Make a left turn at the stop sign onto W. Old Cross Road (Route 211). Use the left lane as you enter town. At the second stoplight, you will see the Strayer House on the far right corner. Continue through the intersection and park in the lot behind the Strayer House or turn at the intersection and parallel park on Route 11. There is also a free parking lot south on John Sevier Road, which is the first intersecting road after you pass the Strayer House.

The Strayer House (sometimes called the Lee-Jackson

Building) was constructed in 1807 by Joseph Strayer, who kept a local store. In 1862, Stonewall Jackson used this brick building as headquarters and reviewed his troops as they passed through town. Jubal Early also used the Strayer property for command purposes in the autumn of 1864. From the late 19th Century, the structure was used as a hotel until its restoration as a historic site in 2005.

Currently, the Shenandoah Valley Battlefields Foundation's headquarters is located in the Strayer House. Inside, you'll find a small gift shop, a historical film and art displays, and a local coffee shop. Though this tour will visit several historic sites in town, pick up a walking tour guide if interested in a more in-depth coverage of the older buildings in New Market.

When you're finished at the Strayer House, return to your vehicle and drive to the site of Solomon and Jessie Rupert's home in 1864.

GPS positions for locations on this stretch of the tour:

Virginia Museum of the Civil War
57 George Collins Pkwy, New Market, VA 22844
38.662619 N, -78.670630 W

Strayer House
93863 S Congress St, New Market, Virginia, 22844
Intersection of Route 11 and Route 211
38.647782 N, -78.671546 W

United Methodist Parsonage
(Site of the Rupert home and school during the war.)
9330 N Congress St, New Market, VA 22844
38.649075 N, -78.670877 W

Standing at the historic crossroads, the Strayer House has witnessed over a century and a half of history. During the Civil War, "Stonewall" Jackson reviewed his troops at this corner in 1862. (skb)

⟶ TO STOP 2

Exit Strayer House parking lot, following the signs. Turn left toward the four-way stop intersection. Turn left on State Route 1002. At the stoplight intersection with Route 11, go right (north). Make the first right hand turn on State Route 1006. You can park in the church parking lot and walk to the site of Jessie Rupert's house or continue driving east on State Route 1006 to visit the additional sites listed in Chapter 2's tour notes.

A "Yankee Dutchman" and His Soldiers

CHAPTER TWO

SPRING 1864

The maps lying on the table and tracing the roads, rivers, creeks, and topography of the Shenandoah Valley were as complex as the man who studied them to formulate a campaign that would attempt to accomplish the directives of his superiors, perhaps winning lasting respect—finally—for him and his countrymen. Major General Franz Sigel had been involved in the Civil War from its beginning, serving in Missouri at the battle of Wilson's Creek and fighting at the battle of Pea Ridge in Arkansas before transferring to the Eastern Theater. In Virginia, he fought under Maj. Gen. John Pope at the battle of Second Bull Run and spent much of 1863 on light duty in the east, away from the armies. German Americans loved Franz Sigel, as did Sigel's men, and the phrase "I fights mit Sigel" advertised their loyalty. Unfortunately for Sigel, his reputation had been greater than his successes by the spring of 1864.

Born in 1824 in Germany, Franz Sigel grew up reading about the life and campaigns of Napoleon Bonaparte. He eventually attended Karlsruhe Military Academy where he spent four years drilling, studying, and formulating strong ideas about his world. He took part in the 1848 revolutions of Germany, actually leading a so-called army of nationalist radicals in several battles and gaining influence among the revolutionaries, despite losing the battles. Defeated and exiled from his home country, Sigel wandered Europe, trying to stay one step ahead of the authorities on his journeys to Switzerland and England. He had read about the land of "Jefferson,

Union soldiers prepared to march deeper into the Shenandoah Valley with Franz Sigel. Their enthusiasm faded as they learned more about their new commander, but they faced the campaign with determination and courage. (skb)

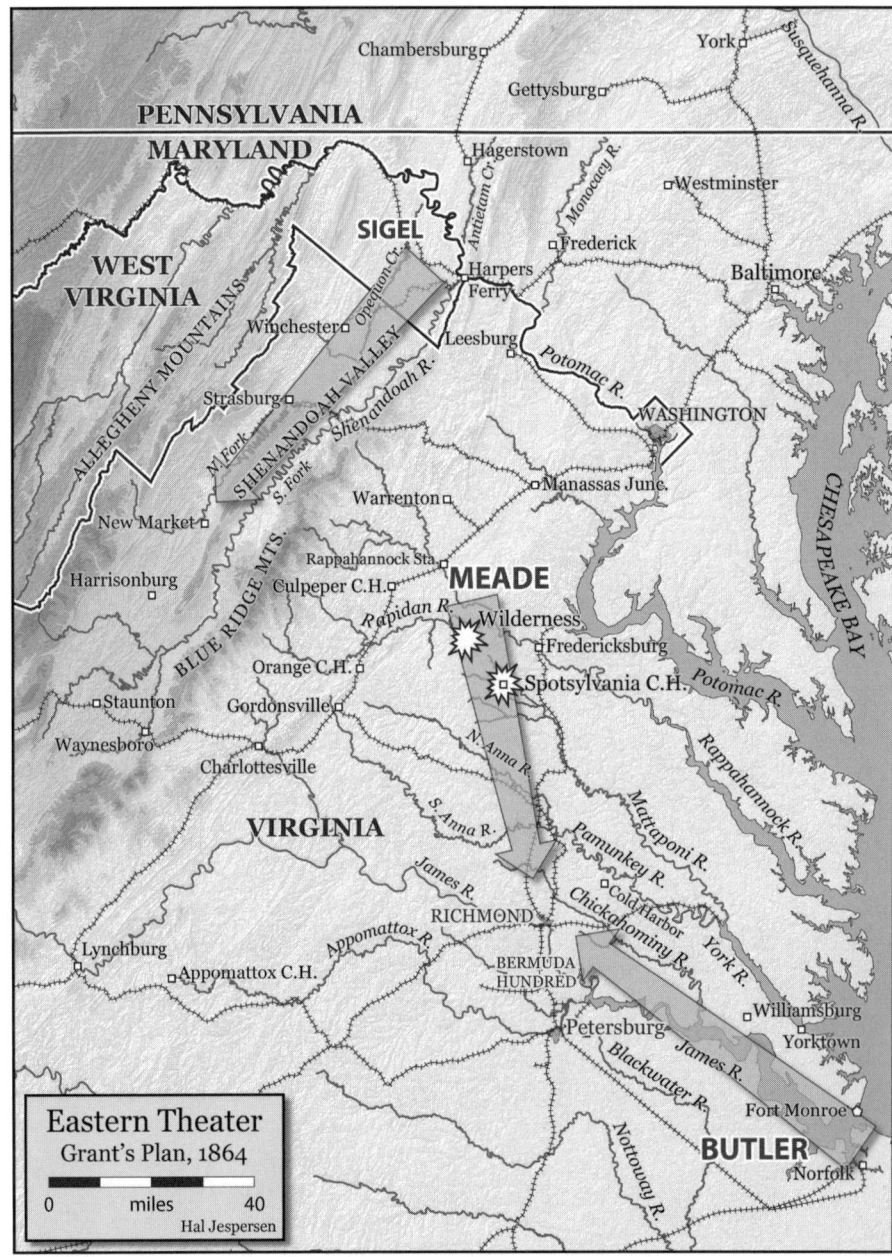

EASTERN THEATER, GRANT'S PLAN—In General Grant's planning, Sigel's campaign was just one Union effort, working in conjunction with other armies to batter the Confederate forces in Virginia and prevent reinforcements from reaching Lee's Army of Northern Virginia.

Franklin, and Washington," and, as opportunities closed in Europe, he made the difficult decision to leave the continent, culture, and ideologies he had always known and endeavored to make his way to the United States.

On May 1, 1852, Sigel boarded a steamer and

embarked for a new land; he arrived on May 15, exactly twelve years before he arrived near New Market, Virginia, to fight a battle that sealed the legacy of his American military service. Twelve years was well in the future, though, when this German immigrant stepped ashore in New York City, seeking work as a tutor and later embarking on a small business venture with other family members. After marrying in 1854, Sigel started teaching at the German-American Institute, also called the Feldner School, becoming a popular and respected instructor. His interest in the military arts continued, and he joined the 5th New York militia, commissioning as a major. By 1857, Sigel had moved his growing family to St. Louis, Missouri, first taking a professorship at Deutsches Institut and three years later serving as a capable district superintendent of St. Louis public schools.

Franz Sigel had much to gain and lose as he began his campaign into the Shenandoah Valley. (loc)

Sigel held strong political beliefs but, though he immigrated with other German '48ers, he did not consider himself a radical. Still, by 19th Century American standards, some of his political stances were innovative to say the least. Missouri—a border state with a burgeoning German population—had mixed politics and accepted slavery. Sigel abhorred slavery, seeing it as a human injustice and finding it incompatible with his view of American ideals. At first he reluctantly joined the dying Whig Party but, when the Republican Party burst upon the political stage, he joined and supported Fremont and later Lincoln. He tended to avoid sectionalism, believing in a larger dream of American freedom and equality; much of his political efforts and activism centered on writing for German-American publications and influencing communities of immigrants who viewed him as a military hero from their original homeland. Ethnicity and politics set the stage for Sigel's role in the Civil War and in the Shenandoah Valley in 1864.

At the beginning of the war, the German press in the North made Sigel a poster-general for the Union cause. Sigel actively encouraged his immigrant countrymen to enlist and fight for the Union, but the attention from the press backfired for him. His retreats and struggles to win a fight in the West brought double-fold doubts and prejudice against him: native-born citizens—many already highly prejudiced against immigrants—expected Sigel to be a military genius because of what they had read in the newspapers, and when he failed to produce noteworthy victories, Sigel's ethnicity and military struggles worked against him. The trouble deepened as German

While Sigel ideally defeated the Confederates in the Shenandoah Valley, Gen. U.S. Grant, his staff, and generals would battle the Army of Northern Virginia in eastern Virginia. (loc)

newspapers, undoubtedly trying to help their hero, made excuses and called for greater military authority and promotions for their general. Less publicized commanders might have survived the defeats and retreats, but for Sigel, the attention produced greater stakes.

Among the common soldiers, Sigel won popularity—both with German Americans and native-born troops. The phrase "fights mit Sigel" inspired confidence. Despite popularity in the press and with his troops, Sigel clashed with General-in-Chief of the Army Henry Halleck and eventually earned his exit ticket from active command after the Second Manassas campaign; he could not wait to be called back for field command and pressured politicians and the press to aid him in that objective.

By 1864 Lincoln, Halleck, and Grant agreed to give the "Yankee Dutchman" another chance to prove his supposedly legendary battlefield prowess. They needed a new commander for Union troops in the Department of West Virginia, and the president needed to retain German voter support as the next election approached. Franz Sigel offered a solution to both problems, and on February 29, 1864, Lincoln instructed Secretary of War Edwin Stanton to appoint the German-American general to command the army in the district that had suffered notorious defeats for the Union cause. Opportunity's door had opened. Sigel had been called back to service with a chance to become the American military legend that his friends firmly believed him to be.

Lieutenant General Ulysses S. Grant displayed less optimism about Franz Sigel and the Department of West Virginia, but Grant handed Sigel a proverbial golden ticket in the large-scale planning, since he was not willing to write off a commander without giving him a fair chance. Grant's 1864 plans outlined simple objectives: view the entire unsurrendered South as a battlefield and pursue the Confederate armies until they retreated or capitulated. The detailed plans ordered Gen. William T. Sherman to battle Gen. Joseph E. Johnston out of Tennessee and into Georgia while Gen. George G. Meade pursued Gen. Robert E. Lee in Virginia. Supporting Meade and the Army of the Potomac, Gen. Benjamin F. Butler would strike toward Richmond

FRANZ SIGEL.
MAJ GEN U.S.A

Sigel had fought and lost some battles during the 1848 revolutions in Germany. Despite losing militarily, he had gained a positive and heroic reputation which followed him to America and gave him considerable influence in the immigrant community. This illustration offers an example of the German-American perception of Sigel: a heroic general, ready to conquer, needing only an army and an opportunity. (loc)

and Petersburg from the Peninsula. In Louisiana, Gen. Nathaniel P. Banks received directions to push forward and capture Mobile, Alabama.   Simultaneous with these other movements, Sigel would advance up the Shenandoah Valley, threatening Lee's flank, capturing a railroad hub, and tying up Confederate troops. Sigel, Banks, and Butler had lesser roles and, using a butchery metaphor, Grant declared, "Those not skinning can hold a leg."

Sigel happily took command, arriving in Cumberland, Maryland, on March 11, and relieving his predecessor, Gen. Benjamin F. Kelley. He then began one of the military tasks he truly excelled at: preparing an army for the field. Unfortunately, weather, illness, and disagreeable orders impeded the progress.

Trouble really began on March 29th when Gen. Edward O.C. Ord received orders to report to Sigel. Ord—a favorite of Grant's from the western theater—was supposed to coordinate with Gen. George Crook and head south through West Virginia, destroying the railroad between Charleston, West Virginia, and Saltville, Virginia, which were important locations for Confederate logistics. Sigel protested loudly, claiming, "All dispositions were made in such a manner as if I did not exist at all." He argued with Ord, forcing that commander to ask to avoid reporting to Sigel and finally to resign. Sigel frustrated Grant by refusing to use proper chain of command and neglecting to guard the Baltimore & Ohio Railroad, creating further mistrust of his capabilities for the task ahead.

Among his protests, Sigel had raised a valid point: the West Virginia terrain made it difficult to move artillery. Grant issued new directives. General Crook would take approximately ten thousand infantry and cavalry and head for Saltville while Gen. Sigel would maneuver seven thousand troops up the Shenandoah Valley. By focusing attacks on the Virginia and Tennessee Railroad and Staunton, Virginia, Grant hoped the Confederates would send reinforcements to those points instead of to the Army of Northern Virginia.

Partially satisfied, Sigel prepared for his advance. Some of his greatest difficulties included protecting the Union's Baltimore & Ohio Railroad from attacks by Confederate partisans, securing a supply line during his advance, and overcoming general unfamiliarity with the terrain and warfare in the Valley. Unprepared troops loomed large in Sigel's mind, and he remained firmly

Edward O. C. Ord had served with Gen. Grant in the western theater. Sigel's leadership and chain of command conflict with Ord did not brighten Sigel's reputation with Grant. (loc)

Henry Halleck was no friend to Franz Sigel, and the German-American did not like the commander either. They frequently clashed in telegrams during the New Market Campaign. (loc)

convinced throughout the campaign that his men needed more training.

His command structure changed several times between the time he took command and the opening of the New Market Campaign. Sigel accepted several German-American friends as commanders, and his staff consisted almost exclusively of former immigrants. While it was a kind and political gesture to surround himself with these comrades, it created a divide and communication barrier among the Union leadership. According to Col. David H. Strother, who served on Sigel's staff, "He has a low set about him, and between him and his staff there was no social adoptation and no confidential relations. He has retained us [non-immigrant officers] at the suggestion of higher authority or rather of public opinion and the result was disagreeable to both parties."

Benjamin F. Kelley had commanded the district before Franz Sigel; his son-in-law, Jeremiah Sullivan, would stay and serve unenthusiastically under the new commander. (loc)

Brigadier General Jeremiah C. Sullivan commanded Sigel's infantry division. This thirty-three-year-old general had served in the U.S. Navy prior to the war and started the conflict as a captain at the battle of Philippi in 1861. Unlike Sigel, Sullivan had experience fighting in the Shenandoah Valley, commanding a brigade at the battle of Kernstown before transferring to the west and serving on Grant's staff. His father-in-law, the recently relieved Kelley, had brought Sullivan back to the Valley to have him guard the Baltimore & Ohio Railroad.

Colonel Augustus Moor led the first brigade in Sullivan's division. Moor, a German refugee from the 1830 uprising, had lived in Philadelphia and Cincinnati prior to the war, fought in the Seminole War, and been influential in recruiting German-Americans during the Civil War. His brigade consisted of the 18th Connecticut, 28th Ohio, 116th Ohio, and 123rd Ohio.

Colonel Joseph Thoburn commanded the second brigade in Sullivan's division. An Irish immigrant, Thoburn had practiced medicine in Wheeling, West Virginia, prior to the war and had served with the Union forces during the 1862 Valley Campaign. In his brigade during the New Market Campaign, the 1st West Virginia, 12th West Virginia, 34th Massachusetts, and 54th Pennsylvania marched.

Major General Julius Stahel corralled the division of Union cavalry accompanying Sigel. Stahel and Sigel had similar backgrounds; Stahel, a Hungarian, had served in European armies, gotten mixed up in revolutions, become a refugee teacher, and arrived in America in 1859. He had fought under General John C. Fremont during the 1862 Valley Campaign and with Sigel at Second Bull Run. Stahel had an unimpressive military record but enjoyed the idea of commanding cavalry and socializing with his immigrant comrades.

Under Stahel and commanding his first brigade of cavalry, Col. William B. Tibbits brought campaign experience to the cavalry leadership; he had served since 1861 and participated in the Peninsula Campaign, Second Bull Run, Fredericksburg, and Chancellorsville before becoming colonel of the 21st New York Cavalry in February, 1864, and, a few weeks later, brigade commander. His cavalry units included the 1st New York Veteran Cavalry, 1st New York (Lincoln) Cavalry, 1st Maryland Potomac Home Brigade (detachment), 21st New York Cavalry, and 14th Pennsylvania Cavalry (detachment).

Colonel John E. Wynkoop, who had enlisted in 1861 and won praise for his gallant actions at the battle of Stones River, commanded the second cavalry brigade, consisting of detachments from the 15th New York, 20th Pennsylvania, and 22nd Pennsylvania Cavalries.

Sigel's artillery totaled forty-eight guns. Captain Alonzo Snow commanded Battery B of the Maryland Light Artillery. Captain Albert Von Kleiser directed the 30th New York Battery of Light Artillery. Two batteries—D and G—from the 1st West Virginia, commanded by Captain John Carlin and Captain Chatham T. Ewing, respectively, would also serve with Sigel's army. Captain Henry A. DuPont commanded the 5th U.S. Artillery, Battery B.

Sigel's assembled troops at Martinsburg, West Virginia, received orders to march. At around 8 a.m. on April 29, 1864, Sigel and his troops started for Bunker Hill and Winchester in Virginia. Thomas D. Evans of the 14th Pennsylvania Cavalry recorded in his pocket diary: "Nearly all the troops at this place moved towards Winchester. Our regiment moved off at 2 P.M. we marched 9 miles and camped for night about a miles this side of Rim Run Hill." The campaign had opened.

However, if Sigel hoped to surprise the Confederate defenders of the Valley, they had their own tricks in store to astonish the "Yankee Dutchman." The roads and land on the maps that Sigel studied so carefully had become the playground of Southern cavalry and partisans who were ever ready to transmit their successes and observations to the new Confederate commander in the region.

Unlike some of the other cavalry commanders with Sigel's army, Col. William Tibbets brought cavalry experience to his new command position in the New Market campaign. (loc)

Finding the Unionists In New Market

Franz Sigel spent his time in New Market on the battlefield, directing troops and artillery. He did not have just one specific headquarters location.

The majority of New Market civilians supported the Confederacy, but one brave couple stood by the Union and did not keep their allegiance a secret. Solomon and Jessie Rupert lived on Congress Street. Prior to her marriage, Jessie had lived in Lexington, Virginia, and been acquainted with Thomas J. Jackson, even helping him teach a Sunday School class for slaves. During 1862, Mrs. Rupert boldly flew a Union flag at her home and an overeager Confederate officer hauled her down to headquarters for a reprimand from "Stonewall." Instead, General Jackson welcomed his old friend warmly, and the fact that Mrs. Rupert was a friend of the Valley's hero raised her reputation a little among her hostile, rebel neighbors.

After the battle of New Market, Jessie and Solomon opened their home as a field hospital for Union casualties. Soon overwhelmed, Jessie went searching for another building to bring the boys in blue out of the rain and make tending their injuries easier. Her neighbors—busy with Confederate wounded and unsympathetic to her cause—refused to help. Mrs. Rupert managed to stop a company of Confederate troops and explained the situation to the captain, who ordered his men to break open a warehouse for the lady to aid the enemy's injured. The men of the 34th Massachusetts, grateful for Mrs. Rupert's efforts and kindness, named her "Daughter of the Regiment," and the surviving veterans stayed in contact with her for many years.

In the post-war years, the Ruperts moved to another house, south on Congress Street. There, they operated a school for African Americans, the first of its kind in the town and a controversial decision. Whether it was taking a step in education or standing in a muddy street to insistently ask for shelter for the wounded, Union-loving Jessie Rupert forced progress and humanity in the town of New Market.

The tour will now visit the site of the Rupert home during the battle (structure no longer standing), Solomon and Jessie's graves, and the location of their post-war home in town.

Make a right turn on John Sevier Road. Continue straight at the four-way stop sign. In about .2 miles, turn left on Lee Street (1007). Emmanuel Cemetery will be on

TOP: Solomon Rupert worked tirelessly after the battle to move wounded Union soldiers to shelter out of the rain. (nmhs)

ABOVE: Jessie Rupert lived the remainder of her life in New Market, challenging her neighbors to accept new and inclusive ideas about their world and community. (nmhs)

the right; use the first driveway beside the church. Pull just beyond the church building and stop.

The Rupert graves are located at the back of the church building. Look for two large, white headstones, about five feet tall. From the Rupert graves, look to the right for the large Crim family headstone.

Return to your vehicle. Follow the cemetery lane, making left turns toward the exit. At the cemetery exit, turn left on Lee Street. At the second stop sign in approximately one block, turn right on Congress Street.

The Rupert's post-war home is located just before the local bank and stoplight.

Continue north on Congress Street (Route 11) from the Rupert's post war home. Turn left on 211 West. At the first signal light, turn right at the hotel entrance. Drive toward the freeway in the hotel parking lot, as far as you can. Park facing south. Shirley's Hill is just on the other side of the freeway, in front and slightly to the right. It is the hill with the water tower on it.

Jessie Rupert lived in this house after the Civil War and operated a school for African Americans in the upper stories of the building, believing in education for all. (skb)

GPS positions for locations on this stretch of the tour:

United Methodist Parsonage
(Site of the Rupert home and school during the war)
9330 N Congress St., New Market, VA 22844
38.649075 N, -78.670877 W

Emmanuel Lutheran Church and Cemetery
155 E Lee St., New Market, VA 22844
38.645824 N, -78.670713 W

Vicinity of the gravestones: 38.645618 N, -78.670815 W

Site of the Ruperts' post-war home
9401 S Congress St., New Market, VA 22844
38.647377 N, -78.672180 W

To view Shirley's Hill: 38.649761 N, -78.673943 W

The inscription on Jessie Rupert's grave names her as "daughter of the regiment" for the 34th Massachusetts Regiment in honor of her efforts to care for their wounded after the battle of New Market. (skb)

An Exiled General and His Gathered Army

CHAPTER THREE

SPRING 1864

The numbers seemed impossible: nearly eighteen thousand square miles of mountains to defend with just 5,175 troops.

John C. Breckinridge had faced pressure before, but the odds were stacked heavily against him this spring of 1864. The pressure to defend an entire military department was far different from the pressures he had endured in Congress and as vice president. There, he had used his voice, reason, and the power of the law to resolve conflicts or simply defer decisions on questions. Eventually, enough political questions had been deferred that war became the means of resolution, and now the answers would come on the battlefield. There, troop numbers, military skill, and casualties—and sometimes a degree of luck—ruled the day. In his new department—which included the Shenandoah Valley—Breckinridge would have to fight with few troops, hoping his leadership, critical thinking, and some much-needed luck could supply what the numbers could not.

Breckinridge thrived on challenges and had experienced a measure of luck earlier in his life. Born in 1821 and shuffled off to relatives at a young age by his widowed mother, young Breckinridge had gained a respect for authority, sense of heritage, and deep sensitivity. Well educated but without a fortune, he turned to practicing law and gained local attention for his public speaking. Breckinridge journeyed west to Iowa before returning to Kentucky to marry and rise in local political prestige. Following non-combat service during

A replica of the famous—or infamous—"Breckinridge post" stands near St. Matthew's Lutheran Church in New Market. While it is unknown if a shell hit a post instead of the general, it is clear that Breckinridge rode under fire during the battle of New Market and took an active leadership role, directing the fight. (skb)

John Breckinridge (left) had a successful and almost undefeated record of political victories. He served as vice president under James Buchanan—the youngest person to hold the office. Following his career as a mustachioed general (right), which would end shortly after New Market, Breckinridge would serve briefly as the Confederate Secretary of War, escape the crumbling Confederacy, live in exile in Canada, and eventually return to the United States. (loc) (loc)

the Mexican-American War (1846-1848), he won a seat in the Kentucky House of Representatives, and in 1851 headed to Washington D.C. to represent his state for two consecutive terms. Breckinridge decided to step away from politics in Washington after his second term, devoting his time to looking after his family. The Democratic Party eventually put Breckinridge on their ticket for vice president in the 1856 election and, when James Buchanan won the executive office, Breckinridge became the youngest vice president in U.S. History.

Politically, Breckinridge supported and represented the Democratic Party, but he was not the fire-eating secessionist that others later painted him as. Throughout his antebellum legal and political careers, Breckinridge opposed Know-Nothingism and nominally supported sectionalism, though he mostly looked out for his border state Kentucky. He owned slaves and supported pro-slavery legislation or rulings, but disliked the institution, hoping compromise or emancipation might eventually be reached but believing that the law must be upheld in the meantime.

In the 1860 presidential election, Breckinridge as the sitting vice president made a run for office. Those were the days when a candidate's party and advisors crafted the platform and organized the campaign, and for Breckinridge, his political platform quickly spiraled out of his reach and beyond his personal beliefs. Painted by the press, supporters, and secessionists as a candidate of choice for the South, the man himself spent hours trying to convince his supporters that he really loved the Union and was not in favor of secession. His campaign managers tried to keep the candidate's views on slavery quiet; Breckinridge hated slavery's cruelties and some claimed that in the early 1850s he had even mentioned forcible abolition.

When election day came, Breckinridge attracted

a mix of voters: some saw him as a candidate for the South, though lacking the fiery rhetoric in favor of secession; others saw him as a candidate to save the Union and prevent Southern secession through some sort of compromise or status quo. In the end, the Kentuckian secured seventy-two electoral votes, compared to Abraham Lincoln's one hundred eighty. Though he lost the election, Breckinridge had pulled his voters from every section of the country—North, South, and border states—and generally represented men who believed a Breckinridge victory could keep the country together.

The presidential election was his first political defeat, but Breckinridge clung to the hopes he had earlier expressed. "Yes, the truth will prevail," he had said. "You may smother it for a time beneath the passions and prejudices of men, but those passions and prejudices will subside; and the truth will reappear as the rock reappears above the receding tide. I believe this country will yet walk by the light of these principles. Bright and fixed, as the rock-built lighthouse in the stormy sea, they will abide, a perpetual beacon, to attract the political mariner to the harbor of the Constitution."

However, the Constitution was the very document attacked and debated as Southern states seceded prior to and after Lincoln's inauguration. Breckinridge—a man of convictions, long misunderstood and misrepresented—came under scrutiny and question. Did he believe in Union or secession? Did he believe in slavery or freedom? Publicly, as Buchanan's vice president, Breckinridge encouraged "moderation, forbearance and compromise" and waited to give further encouragement or endorsements.

An American Flag with Portrait of John C. Breckenridge, encircled by 33 Stars in a Blue Field, bearing the names—President, John C. Breckenridge; Vice President, Gen. Jos. Lane.

This flag is an example of presidential election material prepared for candidate Breckinridge in 1860. Significantly, it is a Union flag with all stars on the blue field—a reminder that the candidate himself was not a fire-eating secessionist, though some of his campaign stumpers liked to portray him that way. (loc)

In 1860, John Breckinridge ran for president against Stephen Douglas, John Bell, and Abraham Lincoln; his running mate for vice president was John Lane. (loc)

In those days when state legislatures still chose senators, Kentucky had chosen Breckinridge to represent her in the Senate, so the day Lincoln and Hannibal Hamlin took office, Breckinridge took a senator's oath and seat. There, he made efforts at reconciliation, waited to see where Kentucky would cast her lot, and eventually accepted the state's bid for neutrality. Back in the Senate, he protested Lincoln's growing war powers and found himself accused of treason as the weeks passed. On the evening of August 6, 1861, Breckinridge said good-bye to Washington during the Congressional adjournment, heading home to try retrieving his oldest son, sixteen-year-old Cabell, from Confederate enlistment.

Committed to state neutrality and abhorring the idea of Civil War, Breckinridge was caught in September when the state legislature abandoned neutrality and sided with the Union; nearly arrested by Federal authorities, Breckinridge fled South, choosing freedom and the Confederacy over arrest, imprisonment, and Union. A principled man caught in bad times and with each side pressuring him to conform to their unconstitutional ways, Breckinridge joined the Confederacy by default, but once there, became an able general and ex-U.S. senator.

Promoted to brigadier general after the battle of Shiloh in April 1862, Breckinridge led Confederate forces at the battle of Baton Rouge in August, then found himself serving under Braxton Bragg at Stones River, Chickamauga, and Missionary Ridge. After Bragg accused him of drunkenness, the exiled Kentuckian needed a new assignment. About that same time, General Samuel Jones, commander of the Western Department of Virginia, was relieved of command. Breckinridge arrived to take his place after a brief time in Richmond attending military meetings with General Robert E. Lee.

The Trans-Alleghany Department, as the tract was also called, incorporated a vast amount of land resources to defend against Yankee attack. Basically, Breckinridge's new department ran west from Virginia's Blue Ridge Mountains through southern West Virginia to the Kentucky border and parts of that state that might be held for the Confederacy. Four hundred miles of border to watch and guard from attack made for a nearly impossible numbers game, given the lack of troops and supplies available in the region. Still, defense was a necessity. The lower Shenandoah Valley fed Lee's army, Saltville produced salt for the Confederacy, lead mines in Wythe County kept bullets in the cartridge boxes, and the Virginia and Tennessee Railroad ran through the district. By 1864, that key rail line had been cut by Federals at Knoxville, Tennessee, but parts remained open and vital to the Confederacy.

This political cartoon from the 1860 presidential election suggests the contemporary opinion of the day crafted by the press and campaign managers that Breckinridge was the candidate for the rebellious South. In reality, the Kentuckian won votes all across the country, defended the Constitution, and was not in favor of slavery. (loc)

General Breckinridge assumed command on March 4, 1864, immediately encountering a problem. Just over five thousand soldiers were available to defend his district, and they were spread out over the area. The general and a few staff officers set out to study the territory and connect with the few commanders before the Union troops made any offensives.

Colonel John McCausland commanded an infantry brigade of about twelve hundred men. A graduate of the Virginia Military Institute in the Class of 1857 and the University of Virginia in 1858, McCausland had taught math at VMI and witnessed John Brown's execution prior to the war. Joining early and recruiting the 36th Virginia Regiment, he had served in Kentucky, fled Fort Donelson, and fought in the Old Dominion.

Brigadier General John Echols had nearly eleven hundred fifty men under his watchful eye. Briefly attending VMI, Echols graduated from Washington College (now Washington and Lee University). After additional study at Harvard, he was admitted to the bar in 1843. Echols had battled at First Manassas and Kernstown before earning his promotion to brigadier general in the Shenandoah Valley. Since promotion, his service and commands had been exclusively in the

John Echols—a native of the Shenandoah Valley—had been active in the region's recruitment and defense since the early days of the war. (vmi)

western Virginia area, and he knew the territory well. His infantry brigade consisted of the 22nd and 26th Virginia Infantry regiments and the 23rd Virginia Battalion.

Brigadier General Gabriel C. Wharton and his troops had been previously detached from the department to assist in the Department of East Tennessee. Wharton, also a graduate of the Virginia Military Institute in the Class of 1847, had spent his pre-war years as a civil engineer and had spent time in Arizona Territory looking after some mining interests. He had fought in western Virginia early in the war, escaped capture at Fort Donelson, and returned to defend western Virginia. Wharton had been promoted to general in July 1863 and had temporarily commanded the Valley District.

The cavalry, under Brig. Gen. John D. Imboden, who oversaw operations and defense in the Shenandoah Valley, eyed the gathering Union troops with six regiments and the aid of several groups of partisan riders. Imboden had briefly attended Washington College and practiced law in Staunton, Virginia, prior to the war. He served with the Staunton Artillery, then organized cavalry units to fight in the 1862 Valley Campaign. Promoted to general in 1863, he guarded the Confederate ambulance trains after Gettysburg on the retreat to the Virginia riverbank. Skillful, capable, and with experience in the Valley, Imboden was well prepared to command his brigade, which included the 18th Virginia Cavalry, 23rd Virginia Cavalry, 62nd Virginia Mounted Infantry, 1st Missouri (Company A), Davis's Maryland Cavalry, 2nd Maryland Battalion, and McNeill's Rangers.

The artillery contingency for the Trans-Alleghany quarter was woefully small. By the time the battle of New Market unfolded, Breckinridge had managed to rally and pull together only eighteen guns, including Chapman's Battery, Jackson's Battery, McClanahan's Battery, and two cannon from the Virginia Military Institute.

With these small and scattered forces, Breckinridge awaited orders and the Federal moves. He did not have long to prepare. Spring awoke the mountains and Shenandoah Valley, promising a season of campaigning.

As Grant, Meade, and the Army of the Potomac rumbled toward the Army of Northern Virginia, Breckinridge received orders from Lee. Dated May 1, 1864—as Sigel's men marched southward—they read:

General: I gather from the reports of scouts recently from the Valley that [Union cavalry Brig. Gen.] Averell has set out on an expedition, the design of which is either to reach some point on the Virginia and Tennessee Railroad, or to effect the capture of Staunton. . . . I think it would be well to have everything prepared to meet him, and, in conjunction with General Imboden, to destroy him, if possible. The enemy will probably make a diversion from the Kanawha Valley to keep your forces occupied while he accomplishes his main design. I am inclined to think that his object is to move on Staunton. If so, you might move against his line of communications while Imboden holds him in front, or concoct some other plan of defeating him. . . . [I]t will be impossible to send any re-enforcements to the Valley from this army. I have instructed General Imboden to communicate with you. A late report from a citizen places General Sigel at Martinsburg, but this conflicts with former reports.

Gen. Wharton was a Virginia Military Institute alumus and had spent much of the Civil War in western Virginia and Tennessee fighting or picketing for the Confederacy. (vmi)

Breckinridge issued orders quickly, calling Echols and Wharton to join him in the Shenandoah Valley to assist Imboden in a defensive fight against Sigel. He left Col. McCausland to defend the Virginia and Tennessee Railroad and hopefully hold off Averell and Crook.

By May 8, Breckinridge had arrived at Staunton, Virginia—located about half-way down the Shenandoah Valley—after enduring a long and wearying ride. Staunton would be the rallying point for Breckinridge's troops to confront the Yankee Dutchman. That town connected the Valley to eastern Virginia via the Virginia Central Railroad, and as the campaign unfolded, it became clear that Confederate victory in the Valley would secure Lee's far left flank, providing some relief during the continuing Overland Campaign.

As Sigel and his divisions advanced slowly up the Valley watched and harassed by Imboden's horsemen, the Confederate general called for the local county reserves to assemble and pondered his miniscule numbers. A company of the 3rd Confederate Engineers joined the gathering force, able to fight as infantry. Still, Breckinridge worried about his battlefield chances and the limited number of soldiers.

Francis H. Smith, superintendent of the Virginia Military Institute, sent a message, offering additional re-enforcements from the school. Breckinridge delayed, well aware that those re-enforcements were trained soldiers but also students from a military school with no battle experience. Many were the exact age of Breckinridge's oldest son, Cabell, who had been captured at Missionary Ridge and only recently returned to his father. The thought of bringing more boys to possible battlefields delayed the general's order.

However, by May 10, 1864, with Sigel inching farther into the Valley and a battle fast approaching, Breckinridge sent a swift messenger to Lexington, Virginia. With pressure mounting and numbers still frightfully low, it was time to call out the cadets.

From Breckinridge's Perspective

A view of Shirley's Hill, where Breckinridge spent the early hours of the battle. (skb)

When General Breckinridge reached the New Market area, Shirley's Hill was one of his first battlefield locations. Perched on that hill, the former U.S. vice president and senator pondered how to fight the battle that would keep the Valley in Southern hands and protect Lee's flank. On that hill, Breckinridge received word that Crook had been driven back, and he decided to attack Sigel, turning New Market from a Confederate defensive engagement to an offensive, forward movement.

A Union soldier remembered, "Loud . . . cheering came from the Confederate lines [on Shirley's Hill]. As I watched a general officer mounted upon a white horse rode slowly down the ranks of gray. He held his hat in his hand. At times he would halt in front of some regiment and apparently from the shouts and yells said something that appealed to their soldierly feelings. I thought of Napoleon in Egypt addressing veterans under the shadow of the Pyramids. As he came opposite our front I leveled my rifle at him but something happened just then that changed my thoughts." Could this be one of the few—if only—battle descriptions of Breckinridge interacting with his common soldiers on Shirley's Hill? It could have been another officer, but the described actions would fit Breckinridge's characteristics and charisma well.

▶ **TO STOP 3**

Return to Congress Street and go north on Route 11; drive approximately two blocks and make a left turn on Breckinridge Lane. Park in the church parking lot and walk to the corner of Breckinridge Lane and Congress Street to see the legendary Breckinridge fence post.

John C. Breckinridge and his staff were the only mounted officers on the Confederate side during the battle of New Market, and they moved around during the fight, directing the battle to the best of their ability and visibility in the storm. According to local legend, the general was at this intersection when a shell nearly struck him, but instead hit the church fence post. It's a fascinating story, but the probability of its factual origin has been called into question by researchers. Today, the post and shell are replicas—a reminder of how local history and memory adds color, legends, and lore to the facts of the past.

A recreated "Breckinridge post" marks the spot of one of the battle's most dramatic—if apocryphal—stories. (skb)

GPS locations:

Reformation Lutheran Church
9283 N Congress St., New Market, VA 22844
38.650765 N, -78.670449 W

The Breckinridge Post 38.650476 N, -78.670213 W

▶ **TO STOP 5**

Exit the church parking lot after viewing the "Breckinridge Post." Turn left onto Route 11, and make a right turn at the first traffic light, taking Route 211 East. Stay on 211 East to the top of New Market Gap, a distance of 3.6 miles.

Look for the Civil War Trails sign (it will be on the right). If you start down the mountain, you've gone too far. Follow the sign's directions to the driveway and park in the parking lot.

GPS for driveway and parking area:
38.642437 N, -78.611257 W

PLEASE NOTE: Chapter Four will offer the possibility for a side trip to the Virginia Military Institute in Lexington, Virginia, which is Stop 4 (although optional for the tour). Directions can be found on page 35. If you are continuing on the New Market driving tour, follow the directions below. The narrative will pick up there in Chaper Five.

The Boys and the Castled Walls

CHAPTER FOUR

MAY 1864

"We were looking upon the shining morning face not only of nature, but of life also . . . framed in a setting of mountain peaks and barrack towers, gilded by the first faint rays of sunrise," wrote John S. Wise, remembering morning reveille at the Virginia Military Institute (VMI) from his cadet years. In May 1864, a shrill fife and drum roll awakened the 284 cadets, summoning them to morning inspection, much to the chagrin of some young fellows who wished to "postpone it till eight."

However, luxury and ease were not watchwords at the Institute or values the founders had wished to instill in youth. Established in 1839 for the purpose of preparing young men to be citizen-soldiers, VMI served a dual purpose: guarding the arsenal located in Lexington, Virginia, and providing a high-quality educational course for young students. Cadets—typically between ages fifteen and early twenties—entered the Institute by application and remained if they were apt students who did not acquire the maximum demerits.

As faculty at a military academy sponsored by the state, VMI professors and instructors taught military discipline, drill, and weaponry in addition to mathematics, sciences, history, and composition. Not all graduates who exited the Institute on July 4—the original graduation day—entered professional U. S. or militia military service; most returned to civilian occupations, often achieving leading roles in their community or state as they grew older. However, having military experience and training as a citizen-soldier gave many VMI

This section of Virginia Military Institute's barracks contains cadet rooms dating back to the Civil War as well as "Stonewall" Jackson's classroom. The cadets would have marched past here as they began their march north to join Breckinridge. (skb)

Founded in 1839, this is how VMI appeared in 1857 on the eve of the Civil War. (vmi)

Francis H. Smith supervised the education and discipline at Virginia Military Institute. During the Civil War, he made heroic efforts to keep provisions and weaponry at the school, ensure the readiness of his students for military action, and balance the need for troops with the fact that families had sent their sons to VMI for education and safety. (vmi)

graduates and instructors important roles in Southern armies during the Civil War.

Cadets in 1864 knew the stories and legends about the Institute's graduates and instructors on the war's battlefields. Towering above the others, Thomas J. Jackson—infamous for his strictness, boring classes, and brilliant artillery drills—was already a revered figure to the young men. Few cadets at VMI in 1864 had personally known the famous Stonewall, but many had been present at the general's funeral in Lexington on May 15, 1863. Other graduates—like William Mahone, Robert Rhodes, Stapleton Crutchfield, and Joseph Latimer—carried forward a splendid reputation for the Institute and inspired those still in the classroom. Some instructors and alumni returned to teach while recovering from wounds, bringing stories of valor from the battlefields and inspiring their eager listeners.

In the previous years of the war, the boys at the Institute had made an important contribution to the Virginia war effort and taken part in several campaign marches. In 1861, the senior cadets had travelled under orders with their professor, Maj. Jackson, to aid in drilling new army recruits. One Richmonder described being ordered about by a "fat little cadet, young enough to be my son." Although facing challenges of age disparity, the cadets helped turn the excited volunteers into citizen soldiers through those hated hours of drill.

During 1862, Jackson—by then a major general—summoned cadets from VMI to act as reserves during the Valley Campaign. Jackson limited the cadets' role to guarding baggage wagons and burying casualties, bringing them close to the fight, but not actually under fire. Toward the end of the 1863, the students left the Institute several times for winter marches when asked to reinforce the Confederates against Union Gen. Averell's raids. Cadet Jacquelin Beverly Stanard—called "Jack" by his classmates—described a thirteen-mile march on "a miserable frozen road" but used the experience to boldly announce his willingness to "stand army services."

Surrounded by war, studying tactics, and coming of age, many young cadets chafed to leave VMI's safety and fight for the Confederacy. Some had served briefly earlier in the war, before officers had realized their age or worried relatives had packed them off to school—or, as some cadets called it, prison. With the signs of spring bursting around them in the quiet town of Lexington, these young men's thoughts turned to war yet again. Cadet Stanard wrote to his widowed mother on April 24, 1864, "every body (or Cadet at least) has been right much excited today, been thinking of leaving for the Army. . . . Remember I will be 19 on the 27th of this month and ought to be ashamed of myself to be here. When you are advised to keep me here as long as possible, people don't know my age, and of course they would not tell you they thought I ought to be in the army."

Francis H. Smith, VMI's superintendent, watched the war and conflict in Virginia with growing concern. Though he knew many of the lads had been sent to the Institute to keep them out of harm's way, he also realized the cadets were a trained military force that might prove useful in the continuing defense of the state. On May 2, 1864, Smith wrote to Breckinridge, enclosing a letter from Robert E. Lee that detailed instructions for the Institute and making a military offer to the new district commander. "The Corps of Cadets numbers an aggregate of 280, of whom 250 may be relied upon for active duty, leaving 30 as a necessary guard to the Institute and as disabled," Smith wrote. "The command is organized as a battalion of infantry of four companies, and is usually accompanied by a section of artillery. It is fully equipped, except in horses, and these are impressed in case of need. We have abundance of ammunition, tents, knapsacks, shovels, and picks, and will be prepared to march at a moment's notice. . . . "

The offer factored into Breckinridge's campaign planning, but he hesitated to bring the cadets to augment his available forces. To him, the cadets were schoolboys. He would call them out, if necessary, but he would wait

"Jack" Stanard as he appeared in 1863. This cadet frequently implored his mother to let him leave school and join the Confederate army, but he also enjoyed aspects of life at the Institute, including comradeship, practical jokes, ice skating, and spying on girls. (vmi)

Samuel W. Booth was about twenty years old in May 1864. Though some cadets were as young as fifteen and some as old as twenty-five, the average age of a cadet at New Market was seventeen. (vmi)

Cadet Jonathan Woodbridge served as cadet sergeant major in 1864, which was the highest ranking non-commissioned officer position in the Corps of Cadets. This portrait was created in 1864 when he was twenty, giving a correct impression of his appearance at New Market. (vmi)

John S. Wise—son of former Virginia governor Henry Wise—had been packed off to VMI to prevent him from running away to enlist in the Confederate army. His many escapades had earned him numerous demerits and a reputation by the spring of 1864. (vmi)

and see if he could muster enough troops from other commands.

On May 10, 1864—the first anniversary of Stonewall's death—Virginia Military Institute cadets participated in graveside remembrance ceremonies, returned to their barracks, and finished the day with evening dress parade. That night, a messenger arrived: Breckinridge needed the cadets. Superintendent Smith took the message and immediately issued orders. Cadet Wise later remembered the moment when the boys awoke to the sound of the long roll of the drum and hastily formed to hear the orders.

There in the darkness, with flickering lights creating shadows on the barrack walls, the cadets heard the news they had been waiting for. General Breckinridge needed "your assistance at once," and the march north would begin in the morning, taking rations and a section of artillery. The boys silently waited at parade rest, "but oh! The beating hearts. Oh! The kindling eyes. Oh! The wild rush of pride, hope, and joy that overwhelmed us as we felt that our hour had come at last!" When the cadets were dismissed, a hearty cheer echoed, and the students rushed to prepare for the coming march.

Dawn came. Lieutenant Colonel Scott Shipp, commandant of cadets, assembled the infantry battalion and started them on their journey north to Staunton. The boys mostly behaved with proper military decorum, but they could not resist stomping on a creek bridge to make it rock and sway dangerously. The cadet artillery detachment left Lexington later in the day, delayed by the necessity of finding suitable horses to pull their cannon and caissons.

As the sun rose higher and the dust increased, marching along the grades of the Valley Turnpike lost its glamor, and the cadets' enthusiasm started to fade. The road's hard-packed surface was rough on the body, creating aching legs and blistered feet. By the evening of May 11, the boys had marched eighteen miles and camped off the pike near Midway. It rained that evening, and some cadets sneaked off to a nearby Presbyterian church, propped open a window, crawled inside, and curled up on the seat cushions.

The following day, marching conditions had changed significantly due to the wet weather. "[T]he roads were awful perfect loblolly all the way and we had to wade through like hogs," lamented Cadet "Jack" Stanard, who had been so anxious to leave school and become

Route 11 follows the Old Valley Turnpike. This particular image was shot near Midway and probably near the first camp of the cadets on the road to Staunton to join Breckinridge. (skb)

a soldier. Even with the road difficulties, the battalion covered another eighteen miles. Lieutenant Colonel Shipp rode ahead to Staunton, reporting to Breckinridge and receiving instructions to encamp the cadets "one mile south of Staunton." May 12th—two days after the orders arrived—the cadets had joined Breckinridge's assembling army.

At some point during their brief stay near Staunton, the battalion marched past a girls' school, and the Institute musician's fife shrilled "The Girl I Left Behind Me." One cadet admitted, "Of all places on earth Staunton seemed to have the most girls, and we were too busy scanning their fair forms and faces to think much of the girls we left behind us." Young, full of life, and caught in the exciting ideal of going to war, the boys enjoyed their welcome to Staunton from the girls and families in the area.

While some flirted through the evening, others took time to handle more serious matters. Cadets originally from Staunton sneaked home to visit their loved ones; Jack Stanard accompanied his fellow cadet Cary Taylor home, and Stanard took the opportunity to write a letter to his mother, explaining, "The Yankees are reported coming up the Valley with a force of 9,000 strong. Our Corps will run Gen. B up to 5,000 may be more. . . . Well

Cadet Jesse Dickinson in 1864. His uniform reflects a typical cadet outfit, which had, he admitted, by spring 1864 "almost ceased to be a uniform, for as the difficulty and expense of procuring cloth increased, we were permitted to wear such goods as we received from home, and in time we appeared in every shade from Melton gray to Georgia butternut." (vmi)

A modern-day view from the parade field at Virginia Military Institute of the cadet barracks. During the Civil War, the drills and discipline learned on this field prepared the cadets for their first battle experience at New Market. (skb)

Edward Tutweiler struggled on the march north; his feet blistered badly, but he determinedly kept up with the corps. (vmi)

darling Mother I have written enough I suppose to relieve your mind as to our destination so I must stop. . . ."

Later, the Confederate veterans and soldiers gathered at Staunton frowned at the cadets. Some were angry that the boys stole the girls' attention while others merely found the cadets' appearance on the march a source of entertainment. Contemptuous mutters and a "taunting chorus 'Rock-a-bye-baby'" angered the teens, but they kept their composure and ranks. A day of reckoning might come when those veterans would be forced to acknowledge the training and determination of the cadets on a battlefield.

Orders came to march farther down the Valley Pike on May 13, and each mile brought Breckinridge's army and the boys from Virginia Military Institute closer to Franz Sigel's Union troops and the possibility of battle.

At Virginia Military Institute

VMI remains an active military school and routinely ranks among the top schools in the United States. It proudly continues its military traditions and holds special ceremonies to remember its history. (skb)

If you are continuing on the New Market driving tour, proceed to the tour notes at the end of Chapter Five for the next directions. Locations related to the VMI cadets at New Market will be visited later in the tour.

If you wish to visit the Virginia Military Institute, it is located approximately seventy-seven miles south of New Market. To reach the Institute in about an hour (if there is no traffic) take Interstate 81 South to Exit 195 (the first Lexington exit) onto US Rt. 11 south. Proceed about 5 miles. Stay in your right lane as you cross the Maury River Bridge and bear right onto Main Street. The tan stucco buildings to your left and right are the grounds of the Institute. Just ahead you will bear right and then immediately take a right turn up the hill onto Letcher Avenue. You will pass through the campus of Washington & Lee University. The VMI Barracks and museum are straight ahead.

Have time and want to travel the Old Turnpike? Take Route 11 South from New Market to Lexington,

Note the bayonets on the rifles in this modern parade and review. The tradition of bayonets at VMI goes back to the decisive moment at the battle of New Market. The statue of General Thomas J. Jackson in the background, sculpted by former Cadet Moses Ezekiel, memorializes Jackson's role as a pre-war instructor and wartime general. (skb)

Most of the cadets who went to New Market did not know "Stonewall" Jackson and had not been in his classes at VMI; however, they knew his reputation and victories and some had witnessed the commander's burial in Lexington in 1863. (vmi)

following signs for Route 11 South through the towns and cities along the way. This route is slower than the interstate but gives a better sense of the road the cadets and armies marched. (Alternately, you could start in Lexington and drive north to New Market on Route 11, taking the route of the cadets in May 1864.)

It is strongly advised that visitors check VMI's website for information about any special events that may limit touring opportunities.

Start your visit at the VMI Museum located in Jackson Memorial Hall (the cadet chapel building). Please obey the directions of the volunteers, staff, and cadets regarding available locations to visit. VMI is still an active military school; use proper decorum at all times and do not attempt to enter the cadet barracks.

The VMI Museum exhibits uniforms, weapons, and artifacts from the cadets who fought in the battle. Benjamin Clinedinst's 18 foot by 21 foot painting of the cadets at New Market hangs in Jackson Memorial Hall Chapel, and some cadet portraits are displayed in

A statue of George Washington faces the barracks and was in place during the Civil War. The first cadets to leave for war in 1861, as well as the boys who marched to New Market, passed under the eyes of this solid statue. (skb)

Preston Library. Between Jackson Memorial Hall and Preston Library, Sir Moses Ezekiel's sculpture *Virginia Mourning Her Dead* marks the final resting place of some of the cadets who died at New Market; the names of all the cadets at the battle are engraved on the monument. A memorial statue of Francis Smith stands in front of Smith Hall at the southern end of the parade field.

While at VMI, take time to notice Sir Moses Ezekiel's statue of Gen. Stonewall Jackson and the four cannon displayed on the parade field. The Marshall Museum is also of special interest, offering displays about Gen. Marshall's life and role in World War II. A statue of Marshall stands along the parade ground not far from Jackson's.

If time allows, check out other sites of Civil War interest in the town of Lexington, including Lee Chapel, Stonewall Jackson House, Stonewall Jackson Memorial Cemetery, and the historic walking tour.

A statue stands at VMI today to honor Francis Smith's decades of leadership. Cadets called Smith "Old Spec" behind his back because he wore spectacles. (vmi)

GPS for Virginia Military Institute:
Jackson Memorial Hall—VMI Museum
415 Letcher Ave., Lexington, VA 24450
37.790241 N, -79.435761 W

To resume the New Market tour, see driving directions at the end of Chapter 3.

Into the Valley

CHAPTER FIVE
MAY 1-13, 1864

On the evening of May 1, 1864, Mary Greenhow Lee wrote quickly across a clean, new sheet of paper, recording what she had seen and heard in Winchester that day. "The Yankees have us now, in sober earnest, though I hope, not for long," she recorded. "Sigel has brought a force variously estimated, only a portion . . . have passed through & are out in the neighborhood of Hollingsworths, except some left in the town occupying the Market House. . . . Large wagon trains have arrived & the Sutlers have taken the stores; so far, they are not to enter a house in Winchester. Their object is to go to Richmond, via Staunton; all who accomplish this end will enter our Capital, with a Confederate escort & all the honors of war. . . . We shall soon see another Banks rout."

Mrs. Lee—an avid journal keeper—was not the only pro-Southern sympathizer keeping an eye on Sigel's advance to Winchester and beyond. Cavalry and partisans flitted in the shadows or lurked on the mountainsides, watching and sending informative dispatches to Breckinridge. Those messages had triggered the call for the cadets to join the Confederate defending force, and Sigel's slow journey up the Valley gave Breckinridge time to gather the troops.

While Mary Lee bemoaned the Yankee Dutchman's arrival, Julia Chase—a Union supporter in the divided, war-zone town of Winchester—cheerily reported, "We are once more under the protection of the Stars and Stripes. Our troops entered and took possession . . . causing much joy among the Unionists but sadness to Secesh."

A rainstorm over the Shenandoah Valley, looking into Luray Valley from the Blue Ridge Mountains. Weather and terrain would prove challenging to Sigel and his soldiers. (skb)

Mary Greenhow Lee kept tabs on Union commanders and troops passing through Winchester, always hoping to see them driven back north in defeat. She confided about her adventures in a war-torn town and private feelings in journals that now offer historians insightful views into civilian experiences. (wc)

Charles Lynch from Connecticut kept a journal through his soldiering years and routinely reflected on the sufferings of common soldiers for the Union cause. (cl)

Sigel consolidated his army near Winchester and sent the cavalry on various scouting rides in the lower Valley. The dispatched cavalry rode out in response to attacks on the Union supply wagons during the first days of the march. Lieutenant Colonel John Mosby's men had descended and wreaked havoc, stealing money, horses, and wagons and messing with the telegraph communications.

Once Sigel and his men reached Winchester, they left supply routes open and vulnerable to Mosby's attack while more danger waited ahead for them. John D. Imboden and his Confederate cavalry headed north in the Valley, anxious to discover whether Sigel was headed for Strasburg or would merely hold Winchester. Far to the south, Breckinridge waited for Imboden's reports, tallying the numbers of troops and calculating the distances to march.

Captain John H. McNeill, another partisan ranger, poised for an attack. Lesser known than Mosby, and operating more exclusively in the Valley region and coordinating with Imboden, McNeill devised a scheme to further annoy Sigel. Imboden, Mosby, and McNeill gambled that they could delay and harass this new invading army long enough that Sigel would give up, get replaced, or wait until Breckinridge could rally enough troops to ably defend the region.

McNeill and his partisans headed west and arrived at Piedmont and Bloomington in West Virginia by May 5. They struck the Baltimore & Ohio Railroad, capturing a train, cutting telegraph wires, and forcing a protective garrison to surrender. Once in possession, the raiders burned railroad buildings, wrecking locomotives and freight cars and ambushing Federal troops. They escaped to the mountains without successfully burning the bridge across the Potomac but after causing enough trouble to create a reaction.

This raid fixed the wrath of Edwin Stanton on Sigel, but the general simply called the situation an "insignificant affair," called out the local militia in West Virginia, and ordered the cavalry in the area to keep better watch. That "insignificant affair," though, further revealed the vulnerabilities of the railroad lines and supply routes and raised the skepticism about Sigel's ability as a commander. Moreover, on the day of the raid, the German-American general had been organizing some unique training exercises.

One of Sigel's greatest concerns during this campaign was the lack of training or supposed lack of discipline among his troops. On May 5, the general varied his soldiers' drilling by hosting a type of wargame. The day passed with confusion of sides, orders, and maneuvers as the regiments moved and "fought" a mock battle around a large tract of land. By the end of the wargame, the general and staff officers clearly had lost control and struggled to communicate because of a German-to-English language barrier. The 34th Massachusetts managed to get lost and was in need of rescue from scouts; the other regiments flopped in their camps, irritated.

This sketch suggests negative interactions between Sigel's soldiers and Southern civilians, giving new meaning to the phrase "fighting mits Sigel." (loc)

After deciding his troops clearly need another wargame, Sigel planned to repeat the exercise the following day, but the colonels refused. "I won't serve under such fools," Colonel George D. Wells of the 34th Massachusetts announced, "and you are a fool if you do." The glorious idea of "fighting mit Sigel" evaporated quickly after these training exercises and the Confederate raids on the supply lines.

Sigel spent the next few days issuing orders to his cavalry and reserves, intent on securing his retreat route in case he needed one. Finally, on May 9, the Union army headed south again. "Tents struck and the army moved southward toward Strasburg," wrote David H. Strother, a resident from West Virginia, artist, topographer, and military officer who served on Sigel's staff, recording his observations of the trek up the Valley Pike. "Graves and dead animals in all stages of decomposition marked the way. . . ."

The living residents along the march greeted the Yankees with hostility and complaints of missing farm animals. The warm, dusty weather did not improve moods, which worsened rapidly as the Confederate raids continued.

With Col. William H. Boyd and the 1st New York (Lincoln) Cavalry as the vanguard, the Union troops skirmished their way to Woodstock by the late afternoon of May 11. In town, they made a providential discovery. As the Confederates left town, they had neglected to take or destroy telegraph messages, leaving valuable

This member of the 1st New York Cavalry may have participated in the New Market Campaign. Don't get confused—there are actually two 1st New York Cavalry regiments in this campaign. Notice their designation as "Veteran" and "Lincoln." (loc)

This modern road near the ridge of Massanutten Mountain near New Market Gap gives an impression of the dense foliage the Union cavalry encountered in some areas. It is probable that the top of Massanutten Mountain had been cleared by 1864, offering a clearer view than the modern one. (skb)

information for Sigel. News that Breckinridge still struggled to rally enough troops in Staunton but was finally prepared to move north rapidly could have given Sigel a decisive advantage in the campaign. However, like Gen. George B. McClellan's response to the discovery of Special Orders 191 during the 1862 Antietam Campaign, Sigel squandered this chance. If he had pressed forward rapidly, Sigel could have controlled New Market Gap and the vital link to the east or moved closer to his objective: Staunton.

However, Sigel waited. He drilled his troops. He worried about his supply lines. He puzzled about how to deal with the partisans behind him and the Confederate cavalry skirmishers ahead. Sigel focused on the problems of his situation, missing the opportunity to make a preemptive strike against Breckinridge, who was clearly still unprepared.

The weather did not improve the situation. Charles Lynch from the 18th Connecticut wrote in his journal on May 12, "wet through. Between the rain and mud we are in misery. Duty must be attended to. We are in the field,

A close view of the old road bed that wound up Massanutten Mountain's east side to New Market Gap. This road used by armies and cavalry columns is now mostly overgrown and almost forgotten. (skb)

the enemy's country. What sleep we can get in the mud and rain doesn't amount to very much, as we must lie on the ground. We are enduring hardships for our country. Very little growling or complaining from the boys." From May 11 to 15, it rained heavily, and Sigel and his troops sheltered at headquarters or in their tents. If the general hoped the weather would hinder the Valley's defenders, he would be disappointed.

Confederate troops had hustled in the rain in previous campaigns, and while Sigel waited, Breckinridge, the Confederate brigades, and the VMI Cadets plodded forward. On May 12, Breckinridge issued directives and established marching order for his collective command. Wharton's Brigade would lead, followed by Echol's Brigade. The Cadet Corps and reserve forces would come next. The ambulances and medical wagons preceded the artillery and supply wagons. Approximately 5,300 Confederate troops—including the artillerymen and the cavalry already observing or skirmishing—had assembled to confront Sigel.

To the cadets, the rainy march north offered

John Mosby (standing, second from left) and his men caused trouble for Franz Sigel and the Union supply trains. (loc)

hardship, but they gritted through, determined to show the veteran troops they could stand the marching trial. The novelty of the campaign also had its charms. In later years, John S. Wise, who had made the march as a cadet, remembered, "Even in the hour of levity the shadow of impending bloodshed hangs over all but the cadet. The new world that has burst upon him; the strange, bustling, outside world, so in contrast with the quaint secluded precincts of Lexington; the bright hopes of the morrow; the joyful thought of real soldier-life, banish fear and doubt. He drinks of this bright sparkling stream like the weary traveler at the desert spring."

The Cadets and Confederates were not the only ones on the march, though. May 11—the day Sigel arrived in Woodstock and the day the Cadets left VMI—Col. William Boyd received orders to take his 1st New York (Lincoln) Cavalry and detachments from the 15th New York and Cole's command to the Luray Valley to scout any happenings on Sigel's or Breckinridge's eastern flank.

Luray Valley lies east of the main portion of the Shenandoah Valley, between Massanutten Mountain—which runs from Strasburg to Harrisonburg—and the Blue Ridge Mountains. This smaller valley in The Valley offered a back-door route to maneuver troops. In the 1862 Valley Campaign, Jackson had pushed his men through the Luray Valley to launch an attack at Front Royal before pressing on to Winchester. Sigel had strategic reasoning to send cavalry to check out the smaller valley and may have hoped that the presence of these blue-clad horsemen would discourage partisan attacks from that area.

By May 13, Boyd's column had been out of communication with Sigel for a couple of days, and after

another attack on the supply train, the Union general worried that this detachment might have been ambushed. He sent out a search party to retrieve Boyd, but the search party ran into trouble with the Confederates instead.

Boyd and his troopers passed through the northern part of the Luray Valley and planned to cross Massanutten Mountain at New Market Gap. Overall, the ride had gone well, with some small adventures but no sign of any major Confederate movements. The cavalry column rode up the road to the crest of the gap "and from a height of a thousand feet looked down upon a magnificent scene. The valley, with New Market in the

New Market Gap as it appears from Luray Valley. This view is similar to what the Union cavalrymen would have seen as they approached the gap from the east and prepared to ascend. (skb)

foreground, lay spread out before them. Just above New Market they could see troops encamped, and farther up the valley toward Staunton they could see a baggage train and a herd of beef cattle."

The question remained: which army did they see? Was it safe to descend from New Market Gap? Would they be routed by an enemy force? Or would they see the welcome sight of the Union flag at headquarters?

Standing In New Market Gap

A trail sign helps visitors find and explore the old road bed. (skb)

Today, Route 211 crosses New Market Gap, but traces of the old road still remain.

After exiting your vehicle, look for the Wildflower Trail sign. Follow the trail on foot for about one block and look for the trail interpretive sign "History Marches Forward." Stop, face the sign, and look to the front and left to see the remainders of the old road track.

The historic roadbed in front of you is where Col. Boyd and his cavalry detachment rode on May 13. Part of the column may have been halted here as the commander and his officers peered into the Shenandoah Valley and debated whose army waited below.

In late autumn 1862, Confederate General Stonewall Jackson led his army through New Market Gap on this road, marching east to join Lee and Longstreet at Fredericksburg. It is said that somewhere

The Civil War Trails sign shares information about Stonewall Jackson's announcement of the Confederate Second Corps in November 1862 at the top of New Market Gap. (skb)

nearby, Jackson announced that his command was the Second Corps of the Army of Northern Virginia—marking a transition in name and command allegiance.

Storms in the Shenandoah Valley can come and go suddenly or last for days. This image of a sunset storm shows a clearing sky—something the Union troops would have welcomed above their sodden camps at Woodstock. (skb)

 **To Stop 6**

Exit the trail's parking lot, making a left turn on West 211. Travel 3.1 miles and make a left turn on State Route 1002. In three blocks, turn left at the stop sign on Route 735 (White Mill Road). In about 0.5 miles, go left on Route 620 (Smith Creek Road).

Cavalry Ahead!

CHAPTER SIX

MAY 13-14, 1864

"Sir, I see men riding through the Gap," announced David Crabill, a sixteen-year-old private in the 18th Virginia Cavalry. It was May 13, 1864, and Imboden's cavalry and reserves waited near New Market and north of town. When news of the approaching Union cavalry ran up the chain of command, Imboden ordered the 23rd Virginia Cavalry and Chrisman's Boy Company to take position east of town and oppose the enemy advance.

Chrisman's Boy Company—one of the Southern reserve units—had been formed of teenage boys from Rockingham County. Called out to defend the Valley, they had been maneuvering with Imboden for the past few days. Now, they rode out to take a defensive post and wait to see if the Union cavalry would descend the steep road.

Above, in New Market Gap, Col. Boyd and his officers surveyed the scene in the valley below, taking advantage of the view and vantage point. They had spotted a wagon train, a herd of army beef cattle, and troops and now debated if their friends or foes waited in the valley below. Remembering that Sigel had ordered him to rejoin the army at New Market, Boyd believed they were Union. His subordinates protested, reasoning that Sigel would never have a supply train out front, and it would be unlikely that he had moved his entire army past the gap that quickly. Some of the men offered to ride down and see what happened, rather than taking the entire column into the valley and toward unforeseen dangers. Colonel Boyd agreed, and a scouting detachment of

Union and Confederate cavalries played important roles in the preliminary skirmishes and fights leading to the battle of New Market—a phase of the campaign generally overlooked. (skb)

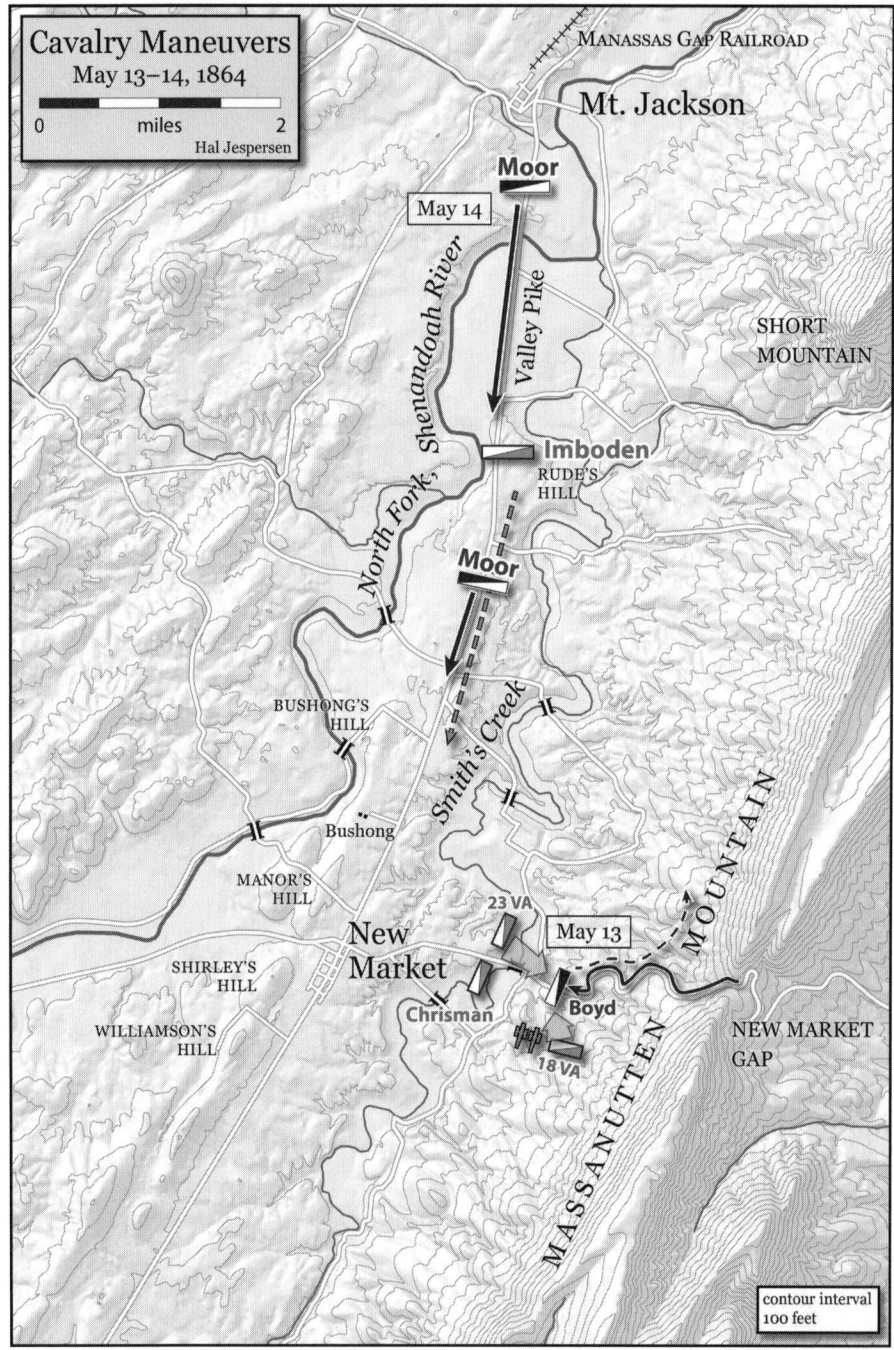

Cavalry Maneuvers
May 13–14, 1864

0   miles   2
Hal Jespersen

MANASSAS GAP RAILROAD

Mt. Jackson

Moor

May 14

Valley Pike

SHORT MOUNTAIN

North Fork, Shenandoah River

Imboden

RUDE'S HILL

Moor

Smith's Creek

BUSHONG'S HILL

Bushong

MANOR'S HILL

New Market

23 VA

May 13

SHIRLEY'S HILL

Chrisman   Boyd

WILLIAMSON'S HILL

18 VA

MASSANUTTEN MOUNTAIN

NEW MARKET GAP

contour interval
100 feet

CAVALRY MANEUVERS—The cavalry contest east of New Market conclusively proved that Confederates already occupied the area and were willing to fight, but whether they could hold it when Sigel's entire army arrived remained in question.

Union cavalrymen descended and reached Smith Creek, which wound close to the foot of the mountain. At the creek's bridge, Confederate pickets fired. The Yankees turned to take back the unfavorable report.

Looking over the fields near where the cavalry fight occurred. The woodline at the base of Massanutten Mountain remains similar to its appearance in the 1860's. (skb)

They had not ascended far up Massanutten when they met Boyd and the rest of the cavalry, which had started an early and uninformed descent. Boyd revised his plan, hoping to keep his horsemen on that side of the creek and, by turning right, move away from the Confederates and back up the mountain slope into the trees, undergrowth, and rocks.

The Confederate cavalry reinforcements moved to intercept the Federal escape, and part of the Union cavalry drew sabers and charged toward the bridge, forcing the Confederates back.

Artillery brought up by the Confederates killed Union horses as the cavalrymen still staggered along the base of the mountain. The fighting intensified, and more Confederates arrived and continued blocking possible escape routes. Finally, the Union survivors—some still mounted, some on foot—dashed up the steep slope, leaving behind dead horses and nearly half the force as casualties or prisoners.

Charles R. Peterson from the Lincoln Cavalry recorded his impression of the fight in his journal:

The modern highway 211 and its bridge over Smith Creek run through the cavalry battlefield at the base of the mountain, along the sites of the original bridge and road. (skb)

In less than ten minutes two heavy columns of cavalry were charging down on us, one in our front and another in our rear. Two pieces of artillery began to send grape and canister at short range through our ranks. Our three hundred men stood firm, awaiting their attack until they were close upon us. Then drawing our sabres we charged the column driving it before us. But owing to the nature of the ground it was impossible to break through. The only alternative was to turn about and charge those in the rear, break through their lines and take to the mountain which was close at hand. This was done. Our loss proves the hardest kind of fighting. I am one of the seven of Company B taken. . . .

Peterson, a prisoner, spent a miserable day in the rain with no shelter before being sent up the Valley Pike on the first stages of his journey to Confederate prison. The Union cavalrymen who escaped up Massanutten Mountain also endured a wet, uncomfortable day as they wandered on foot or horseback through the forest and eventually made their way back to Sigel's army.

The cavalry fight on May 13 proved the Confederates held New Market and controlled access to the gap. Sigel had lost the race to the gap and the success of his march to Staunton remained at stake in the coming battle. With

Imboden and the Confederate cavalry well established in the area and Breckinridge on the way, Sigel's campaign up the Valley—and his success as a general—hung in the balance.

Still, much depended on Breckinridge's arrival with the army. Imboden sent a dispatch: "Enemy is advancing. He occupies Mount Jackson. My advance is at Rude's Hill. I will make a stand here against his cavalry, but if he gets up his infantry and artillery before re-enforcements reach me I shall be forced to retire. Lacey Spring, nine miles this side of Harrisonburg, is the next position in which we should have any advantage of ground. By what hour can I expect support here?"

To the north in the Valley, Sigel advanced some of his troops. With the army still camped at Woodstock—roughly twenty miles from New Market—the Union general sent an advance cavalry force to see what Imboden had done and observe whether Breckinridge had united with the Rebel cavalry yet. The Union cavalry left Edinburg, a little south of Woodstock, and rode to Mount Jackson, a small hamlet on the north side of the Shenandoah River.

On May 13, the same day the Lincoln Cavalry got thrashed at the gap, Sigel directed Col. Augustus Moor to march the 1st West Virginia and 34th Massachusetts

Massanutten Mountain runs from Strasburg to Harrisonburg, and New Market Gap is the only passable gap for columns of troops. This created a topographical challenge for the Union cavalry column and for Sigel's strategies. (skb)

infantry regiments along the pike, following the cavalry advance. Oddly, neither regiment belonged to Moor's brigade, but the officer set off with these unfamiliar units, determining to follow the orders of the supposed German-American genius. Some have suggested Sigel

trusted this German brigade commander more than Colonel Thoburn, who commanded those particular regiments. Whatever the reasoning, his decision and orders created a disjointed command structure after the regiments moved and other units were left without their brigade commander. Along the march, the 123rd Ohio Infantry, more cavalry

Some cavalry units carried carbines in addition to the traditional pistols and sabers. (skb)

under the direct command of Col. Wynkoop, and some artillery joined Moor's already mismatched force.

Early on the morning of May 14, Imboden sent a message to Breckinridge. "Enemy's cavalry were hovering about me all day yesterday [May 13], and I was kept in line of battle several hours," Imboden explained. "Prisoners report their infantry and artillery as under marching orders at 7 a.m. yesterday. I have not been able to ascertain whether they have left Woodstock. The weather prevents observations by signal corps. My opinion is that enemy has fallen back. Will ascertain today and report."

Shortly after, Imboden discovered that the enemy was not retreating. In fact, they advanced, encountering Confederate cavalry skirmishers at Mount Jackson and forcing them across the Shenandoah River. This Union cavalry detachment, commanded by Maj. Timothy Quinn, consisted of the 1st New York (Lincoln), 1st New York Veteran, and part of the 21st New York cavalries. After crossing the partially damaged bridge, they found almost a mile of open fields stretched between the river and a large rise of ground to the south known as Rude's Hill—an open area known locally as Meem's Bottom.

M. Auer of the 15th New York Cavalry later remembered what happened: "My first encounter with the Confederate Cavalry was on the heights about one and one half miles south of Mt. Jackson, after their withdrawal we skirmished on both sides of the pike until we came in sight of New Market."

In the approximate four miles from Rude's Hill to New Market, the Valley Pike rolls over small ridges and ravines—perfect defensive ground for the Confederates. The Confederates used delaying tactics, but their opponents brought more troops into the fight. Wynkoop's cavalry brigade and the regiments under Moor followed, pressing back the Rebels. By about 6 p.m., the Union force had organized into a battle line and steadily pushed Imboden's cavalry south to New Market, through the town, and into a defensive position around Shirley's Hill. Auer explained that when his unit came in sight of the town, they "charged and drove them through the town until our advance was checked by artillery fire. I discovered their . . . formation on Shirley's Hill, on my return north of the town I met a staff officer who ordered me to deploy as pickets, my line extended from east of the pike, west covering the entire front and not more than one half mile from the town."

As darkness closed in, an artillery duel erupted between the Confederate guns on Shirley's Hill and Union cannon placed near town and advancing to Manor's Hill. Eventually, the Union cavalry, infantry regiments, and artillerymen bivouacked in town or near the Bushong Farm, holding positions. If they only had to face Imboden's cavalry, these troops—now miles ahead of Sigel's main army—would be all right. Thus far, Breckinridge's brigades had not entered the fight or been spotted, but Moor and Wynkoop did not know the location of the Kentuckian and his hastily gathered army.

Breckinridge was much closer than the Federals anticipated and had actually issued orders that would bring the pitched battle to the New Market fields if a battle must be fought. Earlier in the day, Imboden had ridden south, believing Colonel Smith from the 62nd Virginia could manage the skirmish, which had quickly escalated. In conference with Breckinridge about ten miles south of New Market, Imboden received decisive orders "to hold New Market at all hazards until dusk" and then trotted back to the town. When he arrived, Imboden discovered that Smith had retreated from the town but arranged a strong position to the south of the village, supported by artillery on Shirley's Hill, which rose just south and west of town, commanding the entire area in a valuable position.

The situation for both army advance forces was less

A pre-Civil War church sits along the Valley Pike in Mount Jackson. A Revolutionary War veteran is buried in the church's graveyard along the Valley Pike in Mount Jackson. The sounds of marching troops would have echoed around his grave in May 1864 as cavalry and Moor's temporary command headed south. (skb)

Cadets remembered Frank Preston's prayer and his calmness in battle. Already a battle veteran, he was one of the few older tactical officers who knew the dangers of combat and was not anxious to suffer another injury or take his cadets into unnecessary dangers. (VMI)

than ideal, but the Confederates had an advantageous position with high ground and two brigades that were already significantly closer than the Union reinforcements. The Confederate army tacked together at Staunton had moved quickly. On May 13, the cadets and other Confederates had left Staunton and reached Harrisonburg. By the time Imboden surveyed the situation as darkness fell on May 14, the boys and experienced troops camped at Lacey Spring, about ten miles south of New Market. Breckinridge pushed Echols and Wharton's brigades forward in the rain and sent orders for the cadets to fall in and continue the march, too.

Despite the continuing drizzle, the boys were convinced that "the dreams of our lives were soon to be realized when we learned beyond doubt that Franz [Sigel] and his German hosts were sleeping within ten miles of the spot where on we lay." The older officers experienced inward concern, though, as the corps prepared for conflict. Captain Frank Preston, a VMI professor and the tactical officer for Company B, had already fought in battle and lost one of his arms. Conscious of the possible dangers ahead, Preston gathered his cadets and offered a word of prayer. "It was not a long prayer," one of the boys later recalled, "nor an elaborate prayer, but an humble, earnest appeal from a Christian, a gentleman, a soldier that sunk into the heart of every man who heard it, and I doubt if it will ever be forgotten even by the scoffer or the infidel. Few were the dry eyes, little the frivolity in that command, when he had ceased to speak of home, of father, of mother, of country, of victory and defeat, of life, of death, of eternity." Then, with the rain muffling drums and shoes squelching in the mud on the pike, the cadets followed the footsteps of the veterans on the final ten miles to a fateful location and day.

In the night, Sigel also received battle reports at his headquarters in Woodstock, and he started some regiments on the march. Charles Lynch in the 18th Connecticut recorded the day in his diary, remarking:

> *May 14. Rain. Broke camp at 4 o'clock this morning. Again on the march, pushing up the valley. Heavy cannonading going on at a distance. By the sound, hot work must be going on at the front. Marching on, passed through the town of [Edinburg]. Go into camp about a mile from town. Our regiment detailed for picket duty. . . . Hot, muggy, wet weather. We are very anxious*

*about the morrow, as we listen to the heavy artillery
firing. We are about fifty miles from Harper's Ferry, our
base of supplies, with no prospect of re-enforcements,
if needed.... Report comes that our cavalry are putting
up a hard fight at New Market, sixteen miles south of
[Edinburg], and about fifteen from our picket line.*

During the night, Sigel ordered the 18th Connecticut
Infantry forward toward New Market, putting that
regiment between Moor and the rest of Sigel's force and
hoping they would be useful reinforcements.

If Charles Lynch worried about the supply lines and
strung-out position of the Union army along the Valley
Pike, it concerned Col. David H. Strother even more.
"Sigel it seems wished to take possession of New Market
to secure the roads leading over the mountains east and
west of that place," he recorded, giving a glimpse of a
sensible though tardy plan. "At the same time this did
not excuse him for sending detachments of his force so
far from the main body as to be destroyed in detail and
to court destruction as in the case of Moor's brigade
which was at this time twenty miles in advance of the
main army."

David H. Strother—
flamboyant, observant, and
opinionated—kept a private
journal that provides insightful
and amusing observations
about the campaign with
Sigel. (loc)

At and around New Market, Moor and Wynkoop
worked their troops into a defensive position in the
darkness, taking a U-shaped position on Manor's Hill.
This eminence rose opposite Shirley's Hill, though at a
lower elevation. During the night, the Confederates tried
the Union line and a firefight erupted, then died down.
Both Union and Confederate troops held their positions
in the darkness while, from both directions on the
turnpike, the sound of marching echoed as Sigel's troops
and Breckinridge's boys hurried toward New Market. In
town, the civilians spent a watchful night while the rain
pattered on their roofs and the stillness was shattered by
occasional rifle shots.

The cavalries had fought. Infantry had arrived. The
commanders and their brigades were on their way. The
coming day would be forever engraved into the local
history of New Market, into the lives and destinies of
the volunteer soldiers, and into the memories of the boys
called out from VMI.

The flat open land between the Shenandoah River and Rude's Hill offered no protection to Union skirmishers from defending Confederates. Interestingly, they were not the first to fight here; according to local stories, a large battle had occurred here centuries earlier between warring Native American tribes. (skb)

Where the Cavalry Rode

Along this drive, the area where Chrisman's Boy Company and the 23rd Virginia fought the Union cavalry is visible. Notice Smith Creek and the slightly rolling hills in this area. The fields today are quite similar to the way they would have appeared in 1864, making this fine operating ground for cavalry. The Union cavalry would have dashed up Massanutten Mountain basically opposite where you return to Route 211.

The pavement ends and the road narrows after you turn left on Route 620. Travel for one mile to Route 211, and make a left onto the highway.

In 1864, the top of Massanutten Mountain at New Market Gap had probably been deforested while the lower slopes still had thick undergrowth, trees, and rocks. The lower slopes would have looked similar to their current appearance, but the view of the Shenandoah Valley would have been much clearer from the top of the gap. This may explain how Col. Boyd and his officers observed the troops in the Valley and how Confederate scouts kept watch on the advancing Union columns from the mountain.

━━━▶ TO STOP 7

Turning left onto Route 211 from Route 620, travel for 1.4 miles and make a left at the signal, turning onto South 11. In approximately two blocks, turn right on 211 West. At the next light, turn left on Cadet Road (State Route 1003). Follow the signs for New Market Community Park, located about .5 miles from the signal light. Drive into the parking area and go to the far side (south) of the parking lot, beyond the tennis courts. Park your vehicle.

GPS for New Market Community Pool parking lot:
9656 Cadet Rd., New Market, VA 22844
38.639986 N, -78.679081 W

The Morning of Decisions

"We had driven the enemy out of the town the night before & were not looking for trouble as we were in ignorance of the fact of the proximity of Breckinridge's forces as we also suppose was the cause with Gen. Sigel," wrote A.J. Gilbert, remembering his morning in position on Manor's Hill.

With his regiment, the 123rd Ohio, Gilbert waited at the center of the Union defensive line along and advanced from River Road, which ran east from the town to the Shenandoah River and over Manor's Hill. The 18th Connecticut and Wynkoop's cavalry crouched to the Ohioans' right while the 1st West Virginia to their left stretched the line into town. Cannon from Snow's battery were positioned in the graveyard of St. Matthew's Lutheran Church and in a slightly forward position. Four cannon from Ewing's Battery sat between the infantry and Wynkoop's waiting cavalry. The 34th Massachusetts Infantry arrived in the area by mid-morning and waited near the Bushong Farm.

Gilbert recalled feeling "much surprised to see about 9 o'clock in the morning the approach toward our line of the solid lines of Breckinridge's troops. And as it was known that Sigel had his force strung out down the valley for several miles and only our little brigade with a section of Battery D with us, it was easy to comprehend what the outcome was going to be."

While his troops at New Market worried about the arrival of Breckinridge's army, Franz Sigel in Woodstock faced an entirely different concern. In a scene of

On Shirley's Hill, Gen. John C. Breckinridge reviewed the situation at New Market—and its context in the larger campaign and war strategy—before making his decision to fight. (skb)

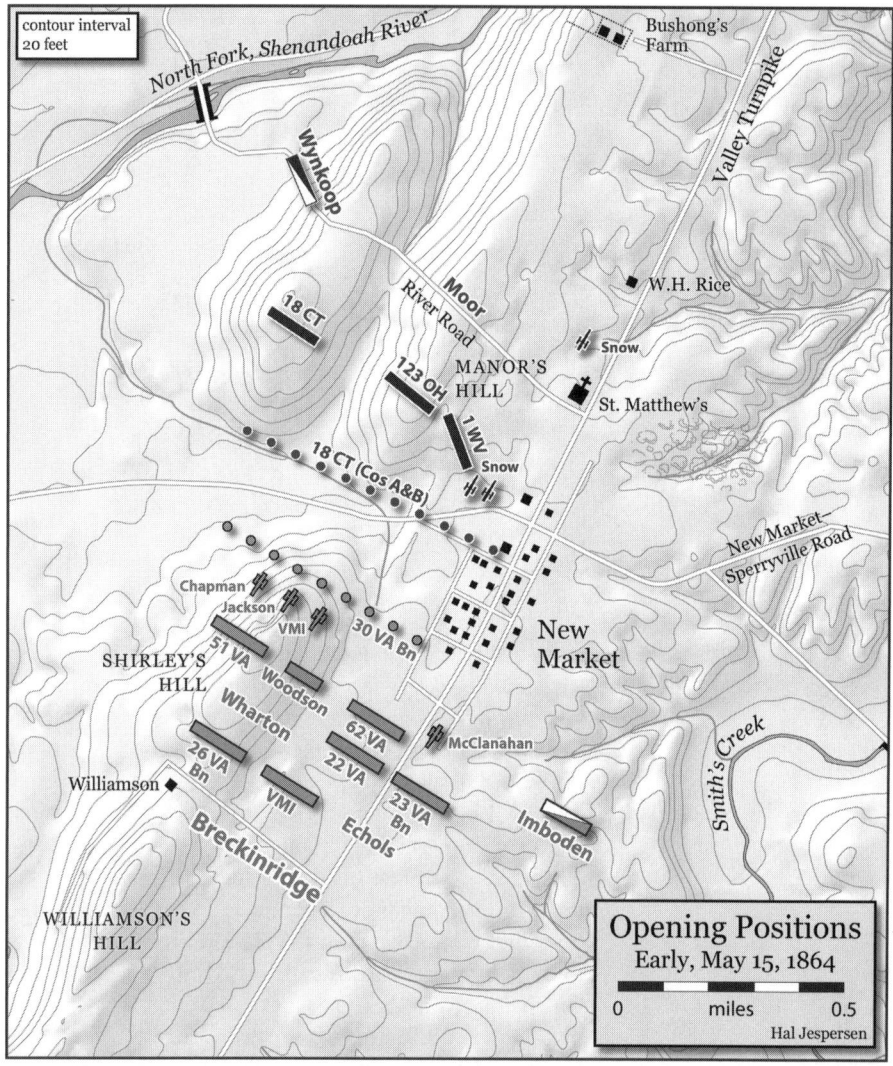

contour interval
20 feet

North Fork, Shenandoah River

Bushong's
Farm

Valley Turnpike

Wynkoop

Moor
River Road

W.H. Rice

18 CT

123 OH

MANOR'S
HILL

Snow

St. Matthew's

1 WV

18 CT (Cos A&B)

Snow

New Market-
Sperryville Road

Chapman

Jackson

VMI

30 VA Bn

New
Market

SHIRLEY'S
HILL

51 VA

Woodson

Wharton

62 VA

McClanahan

Smith's Creek

26 VA
Bn

22 VA

23 VA
Bn

Williamson

VMI

Echols

Imboden

Breckinridge

WILLIAMSON'S
HILL

Opening Positions
Early, May 15, 1864

0   miles   0.5

Hal Jespersen

OPENING POSITIONS—General Breckinridge deployed his men along Shirley's Hill with a line extending east to cover the Valley Pike. Using the topography, he sheltered his troops from direct fire as they waited while also convincing the Yankees he had significantly more troops than he did. Meanwhile, Col. Moor and Gen. Stahel straightened their own lines along Manor's Hill and toward the outskirts of town, adding units that hurried up the Valley Pike to the Union position.

preparation with struck tents and busy packing, "General Sigel came out of the house at a full run toward the camp of teamsters and Negro servants. His high boots were hanging down and altogether he cut a very absurd figure as he ran, exclaiming at every jump, 'By Got, I vill catch dot dam tief.' It seems that in moving he had lost a favorite brandy flask and was accusing everyone he met of stealing it."

Sigel was not the only person having uncomfortable

Looking across the south part of Shirley's Hill and toward Williamson's Hill, this area is where the Confederate troops formed and waited. The cadets and the baggage wagons would have been a little farther back in the beginning. (skb)

interactions that morning. The VMI Cadets marched up the pike early on the morning of May 15, passing Wharton's brigade, which was breakfasting along the road. The boys' solemn appearances in the pre-battle dawn prompted teasing from the campaigning veterans. Surprisingly, the jokes from the soldiers did not irritate the cadets; rather the jokes about coffins and "beautiful corpses" pulled many of the boys from their fears and brought back the more lighthearted perspective on mortality. Others buried their fears deeper, like "Jack" Stanard who had admitted the previous evening to his friend John S. Wise that he thought he would die in the coming battle; Wise had tried to brush off the idea and bring his friend to a more cheerful frame of mind. That morning with both Wise, Stanard, and two other cadets detailed to guard the corps' wagons, it seemed they would be safe no matter what happened.

The cadets moved off the pike just as they rounded the road's bend and New Market came in sight. Moving left, they fell into a reserve position as Breckinridge and the staff officers organized the Confederate line.

G.W. Dunford from the 51st Virginia remembered the early march to New Market after the long, weary trek from farther south. He recalled the artillery going into position first while his regiment waited out of sight and probably had breakfast, joshing the newly arrived cadets.

Shirley's Hill as seen from Manor's Hill. Notice the tree and bush covered side of Shirley's Hill and its open front; these topographical features played a role in how the Confederates advanced.
(skb)

As near as Dunford could tell, he thought his unit went into position on Shirley's Hill by about 9 a.m.—although many soldiers' recollections about timing would prove confusing and contradictory—and he described the scene unfolding below and in front:

> *[W]e were ordered to lay down just outside of a cedar thicket on a northwest slope. Co B and part of the next co was in the open there for the first time we saw the enemy about 300 yds in our front or a little to the left about 1000 strong or as it appeared a full regiment moving in a hollow square as if on drill in perfect formation. . . . I was eager to fire thinking I could have picked off any man in the bunch. . . .*

Atop Shirley's Hill, Chapman's and Jackson's batteries, totaling ten cannon, had rolled into position, and VMI's artillery section, with two cannon and thirty-five cadets, joined them. McClanahan's Battery with six guns positioned on the east side of the Valley Pike aligned with the hill, creating a line of artillery and crossfire. The artillery engaged Snow's Federal guns posted in the churchyard and near the road between Shirley's Hill and Manor's Hill.

Breckinridge lined up his infantry, carefully using

Shirley's Hill and Williamson's Hill to obscure them from Yankee view. The 30th Virginia Battalion from Wharton's Brigade deployed on the north face of Shirley's Hill, below the artillery, visible to the Union as a skirmish line. The 51st Virginia—also belonging to Wharton's Brigade—positioned on the far left flank of the Confederate infantry line on Shirley's Hill, as Dunford described. To their left, Woodson's Missouri Company waited, dismounted, and prepared to fight on foot for the day. Men from the 62nd Virginia Mounted Infantry, now dismounted, completed the right flank on Shirley's Hill.

Echol's Brigade tucked behind the topography in the early morning dispositions, with the 22nd Virginia Infantry behind the 62nd Virginia, while the 23rd Virginia Infantry lined up beside the 22nd across the Valley Pike. The 26th Virginia Regiment waited in reserve with the VMI Cadets. John Imboden and his cavalry—no secret to the Yankees—stationed themselves east of the pike and to the right of McClanahan's guns, ready to advance or go scouting as needed.

Breckinridge had won the race to a battlefield. All his available fighting troops and reserves were on the field by the morning of May 15. For now, the 26th Virginia, the Corps of Cadets, and the county emergency troops

The town of New Market— though larger today than in the 1860s—is still clearly visible from the top of Shirley's Hill. Union artillery in town and Confederate artillery on this hill dueled in the morning hours of May 15. (skb)

formed his reserves. Occupying a relatively strong defensive position, the Confederate general waited, considering the situation and delaying to see if the Union boys would attack him.

Breckinridge knew the situation extended beyond what he could see from Shirley's Hill. Somewhere in his campaign possessions was a message from Robert E. Lee, written the previous day. Breckinridge probably did not need the paper in his hand to remember its wording: "If you can drive back the different expeditions threatening the Valley it would be very desirable for you to join me with your whole force." Clearly, all was not well east of the Blue Ridge with the Army of Northern Virginia.

Looking over the west side of Shirley's Hill, it is easy to understand why the Confederates did not attempt to maneuver troops on this rough and steep terrain. (skb)

Elsewhere, in the mountains to the west, another Union force had penetrated deep into Breckinridge's military department, pushing toward Saltville. A limited Confederate force would meet them some time, somewhere. If that Union force was victorious, Breckinridge would have another problem aside from Sigel and the urgent message from Lee. With these unseen situations unfolding, the general held to his original plans to wage a defensive campaign and battle. If Sigel and the Union boys wanted a fight, they could attack.

Still concerned about his limited forces, Breckinridge employed military posturing throughout the morning. He cleverly moved regiments forward and back on Shirley's Hill, letting the Union officers and troops see Rebel units come and go, persuading them that he had more men than he really had. The plot worked, and many Union soldiers grossly overestimated the number of Confederates in the New Market fields. The ex-politician pulled off some classic military trickery that would have made a Napoleonic student proud.

Colonel Moor decided to hold his own position, growing increasingly nervous as the early hours passed. From the Rebel troops he could see, he realized Breckinridge's flanks outreached the Union position, and the Kentuckian's position on Shirley's Hill dominated the area. Urgent messages were couriered back to General

Sigel until the Confederate artillery caught the range of the galloping messengers. Units continued to arrive haphazardly, tired and hungry from a night on the road. Von Kleiser's battery arrived and joined the other artillery units in the big gun duel.

As Breckinridge lined up and shuffled his troops that morning, Maj. Gen. Julius Stahel and his Union cavalry appeared in New Market. Stahel outranked Moor and took command of the fight, allowing Moor to return to his regiments. The flashy cavalryman apparently liked the position Moor had prepared and did not rearrange the troops. However, he worried about the developments and sent more messengers, asking Sigel to hurry.

From this position halfway down Shirley's Hill, Confederate skirmishers could have seen Breckinridge maneuvering his tropps to confuse the Yankees. (skb)

By lunchtime, Franz Sigel, his staff, and more troops had crossed the Shenandoah River and halted at Rude's Hill, where, with the aid of field glasses, he looked toward the artillery fight at New Market. "Pushing forward from this point [Rude's Hill] we presently reached Colonel Moor's position on a hill at the right of Dr. Rice's house at the northern extremity of New Market," recorded Colonel Strother about Sigel's arrival on the battlefield to assume his rightful command. "Stahel was on the right with a portion of his cavalry, while a battery on the hill [Manor's Hill] was exchanging shots with the enemy's artillery posted on an opposing hill [Shirley's Hill] at the other end of town. Having communicated with Moor, Sigel left his staff near Rice's house and rode forward to reconnoiter. While he was absent, a number of shells whistled over our heads. This was about midday."

Those whistling shells had frightened the town's civilians. With Union artillery posted in the Lutheran churchyard on the west side of town, Confederate shot and shell aimed at that position accidentally hit homes. New Market's citizens took refuge in cellars or neighbors' houses farther from the line of fire. Perry A. Cook thought the artillery shells sounded like "a circular saw running through a dry plank" and later said that one of these projectiles exploded in the Soxman Family's cellar. With two armies maneuvering into positions and an artillery barrage, the civilians realized they were caught in a battle and wondered who would win and what the aftermath would be.

Around noon, Breckinridge made a fateful decision. If the enemy would not attack, then he would launch his force into the battle. In his pocket—perhaps literally, certainly figuratively—Breckinridge had a key communication. Received that morning probably while he lined up the troops, the report from his assistant adjutant general altered the strategic situation. The small Confederate units had repulsed Union Gen. Averell's cavalry raid toward the railroad, forcing those Yankees to retreat. Now, the southwestern part of the military department remained securely in Confederate hands. Only Sigel stood in the way of General Lee's request to come east. Feeling more confident after the morning's dispatch, Breckinridge ordered his officers to prepare for an advance. He instructed Wharton, Echols, and the regimental commanders to dismount. Only Breckinridge and his staff would be mounted in this battle, giving them better mobility and keeping the brigade and regimental leaders close and focused on their own units. The ground could be treacherously soggy after the hours of rain, and the clouds showed no sign of a sunny breakthrough.

Growling thunder evidenced the natural conflict in the sky, out-rumbling the artillery voices below. With his main infantry line now spread out, Breckinridge gave the orders to advance, and his veterans rose up, crested the top of Shirley's Hill, and came into full sight along the pike. The day of battle—long feared or anticipated— had come and the victor would be determined in the coming hours of storm.

At the Confederate Line

If you face the tennis and basketball courts and look northwest, across Interstate 81, you'll see Shirley's Hill; it has a water tower on it. Walk to adjust your location to look southwest (toward the baseball fields). Across the interstate, you'll see a hill with a large brick house; this is Williamson's Hill.

On the now-visible south side of Shirley's Hill, Breckinridge organized his regiments and kept them hidden and sheltered until the right moment. Williamson's Hill was also used to organize troops and the closer supply and ammunition wagons.

Walk to the pool house in the park. If you're in the parking lot facing the pool, look left and note the golf course. Here, in the area of the park and across Route 11 at the modern-day golf course, Echols positioned his men when they prepared to advance in view of the Union troops.

When finished, return to your vehicle to continue the tour.

This photograph looks toward Route 11 from the community pool's parking lot. In this area, across the road, and on the modern day golf course, John Echols positioned his brigade of Confederates. (skb)

━━━▶ **TO STOP 8**

Exit the community park, and stay straight on Cadet Road to return to Route 211. At the stoplight, make a left turn on 211 West. In .2 miles, turn left on Route 619 (Miller Lane); there is no turn lane—please be extra cautious. Follow Miller Lane south, observing Shirley and Williamson Hills. Turn around in approximately 1 mile at Route 779, before the pavement ends. Return the way you came.

GPS for entrance to Miller Lane:
38.648009 N, -78.678018 W

"Battle as Boys Dream Of"

CHAPTER EIGHT
MAY 15, 1864—MID-DAY

"The enemy in three strong lines now issued from the woods and charged down the hill at double-quick, his skirmishers also increasing their speed, and driving ours more rapidly," reads the official report of the 18th Connecticut, describing the Confederate advance down Shirley's Hill. It was the moment that had worried Brig. Gen. Wharton, but his men and the attached dismounted cavalry managed to escape the dreaded fate.

Prior to the forward movement, Wharton had examined the topography his troops would encounter. The north face of Shirley's Hill was open. Where his left flank rested, trees offered protection and a treacherously steep drop-off, impassible for ranks of soldiers. Marching around the left of the hill simply was not practical in Breckinridge's plans or with the position of Union artillery on Manor's Hill. His veterans had to crest the ridge and move in the open down the long slope. In the little valley between the two hills, the infantry would be sheltered from artillery, but in danger from the enemy infantry. In the ravine, which stretched east to join Indian Hollow and the Shenandoah River beyond, a small spring-fed creek ran. Manor's Hill rose from the creek bed and hollow; there, the Union skirmishers and regiments waited.

Wharton had issued specific orders for his advance down Shirley's Hill. Speed was a necessity. The longer the soldiers dallied on the open slope, the more artillery fire they would face.

The general later remembered the advance. "We

A natural, spring-fed creek runs between Shirley's and Manor's Hills. This waterway marked the boundary between the Confederate and Union lines early in the battle and was a threshold for the advancing Southerners to cross. Cattails and other water-loving plants still grow along the waterway, and in some postwar map sketches, artists actually drew in clumps of cattails. (skb)

This is a modern view of Shirley's Hill from the low ground. The lower trees on the hill were not there during the battle, creating a long open slope for Wharton's men, the reserve, and the cadets to cross before reaching relative safety in the hollow. (skb)

passed over the . . . slope of Shirley's Hill and entirely out of sight of New Market, except a faint view from hollow where we stripped [knapsacks and extra gear]," he wrote. "The first bloodshed I saw was on the North Western slope of Shirley's Hill about 300 or 400 yards south of hollow from an exploded shell. . . . [W]hen we reached the top of the hill in front of the enemy's guns I saw no skirmishers in our front and supposed Clark's men [30th Virginia Battalion] had made a flank movement to our left and nearer the river where they would have been out of our sight."

C.H. Richmond, a soldier of the 18th Connecticut on Manor's Hill waiting as a skirmisher, described the moment when there

> began to advance in our direction a line of Confederate skirmishers, closely followed by their support which I have since learned was the 'Corps of Cadets.' As soon as the Confederate support came in sight we were ordered to fall back, which we did in perfect order and under fire from the Confederate skirmish line. Just previous to our getting the order to fall back some of the force opposed to us [probably the 30th Virginia] had taken possession of a barn at the foot of and between the two hills and a shot from this barn killed Capt Spaulding who was in

command of my company. We fell back to the remainder of the regiment. . . .

With the Union skirmishers retreating, the Confederate line from Shirley's Hill pressed forward. To their east, Echols also advanced along the pike. The Union troops and artillery started falling back to a disjointed line along River Road and behind the crest of Manor's Hill. River Road stretched from the Valley Pike running through town, passed St. Matthew's Lutheran Church where the artillery sat, up and over the center of Manor's Hill, and on to the Shenandoah River. As the Confederate troops advanced, the reserve units needed to follow.

With a real battle actually happening, Cadet John S. Wise could not bear the idea of guarding the wagons at the "bend in the pike." From an oratory perch on the hated wagon, he addressed his fellow guards—Cadets Washington F. Redwood, "Jack" Stanard, and Pierre W. Woodlief. "Gentlemen, the enemy is in our front; we are about to engage him," he said. "I like fighting no better than anybody else, but I have an enemy in my rear as dreadful as any before me. In the front we may or may not be hurt, but if I go home and tell my father that I never went into this action, there is no doubt as to my fate. *I*

The cadets marched over this ground between Williamson's and Shirley's hills before cresting the rise and coming under fire. (skb)

Cadet Oliver Perry Evans
was nearly twenty-two at the
battle of New Market. Standing
about six feet, two inches,
he conspicuously carried
the Institute's banner during
the fight, and many of his
comrades remembered Evan's
boldness and enthusiasm. (vmi)

OPPOSITE: The white,
emblazoned flag carried by
the Corps of Cadets provided
confusion to some of the
soldiers and civilians who
firmly believed a French
contingency had finally
arrived to fight with the
Confederacy. The original VMI
flag was dismantled by the
cadets during Hunter's Raid
in June 1864, but this replica
was painstakingly recreated.
(vmi)

know he will kill me, with worse than bullets—ridicule. I shall go at once. Any one who chooses to remain may do so." Unsurprisingly, the three followed Wise, and they joined the corps just as the cadets prepared to follow Wharton's brigade over Shirley's Hill.

Breckinridge rode to the cadets, accepting their cheers graciously. "Young gentlemen, I hope there will be no occasion to use you," he said, "but if there is, I trust you will do your duty." The cadets would follow Wharton's brigade and the 26th Virginia Battalion, the other reserve unit. The brigadier general had ordered his reserves to "conform their movements to mine," indicating he expected them to make a rush down the hill "without regard for order." Whether Lt. Col. Shipp received those orders or had any inkling of the ground his cadets would cross remains a question.

It was the moment the boys had waited for. War! At last. "At-ten-tion-n-n! Battalion forward! Guide Center-r-r," Shipp bellowed. Later, they would remember the moment:

Up the slope we started. From the left of the line, Sergeant-Major Woodbridge ran out and posted himself forty paces in advance of the colors, as directing guide, as if we had been upon the drill ground. That boy would have remained there, had not Shipp ordered him back to his post; for this was no dress parade. Brave Evans, standing six feet two, shook out the colors that for days had hung limp and bedraggled about the staff, and every cadet leaped forward, dressing to the ensign and thrilling with the consciousness that this was war.

The scene at the top of the hill thrilled the boys. The view had cleared enough to see the battle lines. Cadet John S. Wise's wish came true. "Oh! it is a grand sight," he would later remember. "Just such a sight of battle as boys dream of—such as are shown in battle paintings."

The dream lasted only a moment, though.

Wharton's line and the 26th Virginia Battalion made the dash down hill with few casualties before the Union artillerymen found the range of Shirley's Hill's front slope. However, by the time the cadets crested the hill in close formation and moving at a solemn, parade marching time, "the Yankee gunners had gotten the exact range, and their fire began to tell on our line with fearful accuracy. It was here that Captain Hill and others fell. . . ."

On the west side of New Market, the Clinedinst

family's home had a back porch facing toward Shirley's Hill. Twenty-six year old Eliza Clinedinst came to the door when her young brother called and saw a sight she never forgot. "I saw the charge down the hill, and that terrible shell explode right in front of the line as you came down the hill," she recalled, years later while writing to one of the veteran cadets. "You did not scatter

Surgeon Robert L. Madison and his assistants traveled with the Corps of Cadets and took care of the wounded during and after the battle. Madison later returned to Lexington, continued his practice, and tended to Robert E. Lee when that officer moved to Lexington. (vmi)

Eliza Clinedinst—better known as Lydie—saw the cadets march down Shirley's Hill and became one of the first civilians to venture onto the battlefield to help care for the wounded. She became acquainted with many of the "New Market Cadets" and became known as "Mother Crim" for her devotion to them and their memory. (vmi)

and run but closed up the gap made by fallen comrades and elbow to elbow marched down. . . ." At first, Eliza and other civilians thought the disciplined unit with the white flag was long-awaited French reinforcements for the Confederacy.

The exploding shell wounded a few cadets and knocked down many others with its force. Among the injured, eighteen year old Cadet James L. Merritt fell on Shirley's Hill; "while going across a field . . . a piece of shell . . . knocked me about ten feet" and pierced "the lower part of my stomach. . . . I thought the wound was mortal." Cadet Captain Govan Hill went down stiffly with a skull fracture. A shell piece cut Cadet Charles Read above the eye and struck his gun barrel, forcing it to a right angle.

Cadet John S. Wise, who had been so anxious to avoid ridicule, had his own terror: "But, oh Lord! Thunder, lightning, fire, earth-rocks. The sky whirls round. I stumble. My gun pitches forward. I'm on my knees. Sergeant Cabell looks at me sternly, pityingly, and passes on. I know no more."

The sight of blood and cries from injured comrades affected the boys, but the cadet officers took charge, ordering them to close ranks and march forward. At parade step, they continued down the hill, catching the attention of some Union troops and the veterans who had mocked them. In the hollow, they were sheltered from the artillery and paused while the fighting regiments pressured the Union troops again.

The Virginia Military Institute Cadets had endured their baptism of fire. Now they knew the effects of artillery on troops in open fields.

They removed their marching packs and extra gear, leaving it near the creek in the hollow. If they had to follow again or fight, they needed to be ready.

The cadets had been studying war, so it had been on their minds for weeks or months before their chance for glory at New Market. Cadet "Jack" Stanard had illustrated a startling Napoleonic scene in his notebook of dying soldiers, a gallant officer, and a cannon. (vmi collection, photography by skb)

At Shirley's Hill and Williamson's Hill

This location offers a closer look at Shirley's Hill and Williamson's Hill. The topography here is virtually unchanged, except for the modern road and gas station. The slope that Wharton's men and the cadets crossed is clearly visible. Shirley's Hill itself is preserved but is not currently open to the public, and please respect the private residences on Williamson's Hill.

⟶ TO STOP 9

At the intersection of Miller Lane and 211, continue straight ahead onto George Collins Parkway (Route 305). In about one block, take the second left—a driveway for a hotel entrance. Turn around at New Market Lighthouse Tabernacle's front driveway circle and face south. You are now on Manor's Hill, looking at Shirley's Hill.

GPS for Lighthouse Tabernacle:
9394 George Collin Pkwy
New Market, VA 22844
38.651453 N, -78.676668 W

Colonel Moor's Difficulties

CHAPTER NINE

MAY 15, 1864—EARLY AFTERNOON

Colonel Augustus Moor found himself caught in a web of mismanagement and battle by mid-day on May 15. He probably felt some responsibility and personal investment in the fight for two practical reasons. First, he had been the senior commander on the battlefield before Stahel and Sigel arrived and had initially placed the troops in a reasonably strong position that might have held with reinforcements. Second, as a German-American, his destiny in the war would now be somewhat aligned with Sigel's success or failure since he had been part of the gathered immigrant officers attracted to the Yankee Dutchman's independent command.

With the Confederate advance forcing back the 18th Connecticut and 123rd Ohio, Moor obeyed orders and withdrew these regiments "some 800 yards to the rear of my first position" and formed the infantry "on the right of a battery." Now aligned near River Road and with Von Kleiser's battery in the church yard, Moor discovered that these infantry units occupied awful positions and lacked sufficient numbers of field officers.

"The new position of the regiment was most unfortunate for its efficiency, being in a lane backed by barns and two rows of fences," Maj. Peale from Connecticut reported. "A continuous rain of five days had rendered traveling on other than the roads extremely difficult, and the men stood knee deep in mud. As the lane was entered by the flank, so nothing but a flank movement could extricate the regiment in order." The Ohioans faced a similar difficult position.

In 1864, River Road ran from the Valley Pike up Manor's Hill and to the Shenandoah River. The farm lane offered a prepared line for Union troops to retreat to after the Confederates pushed them off the south-facing slope of Manor's Hill. (skb)

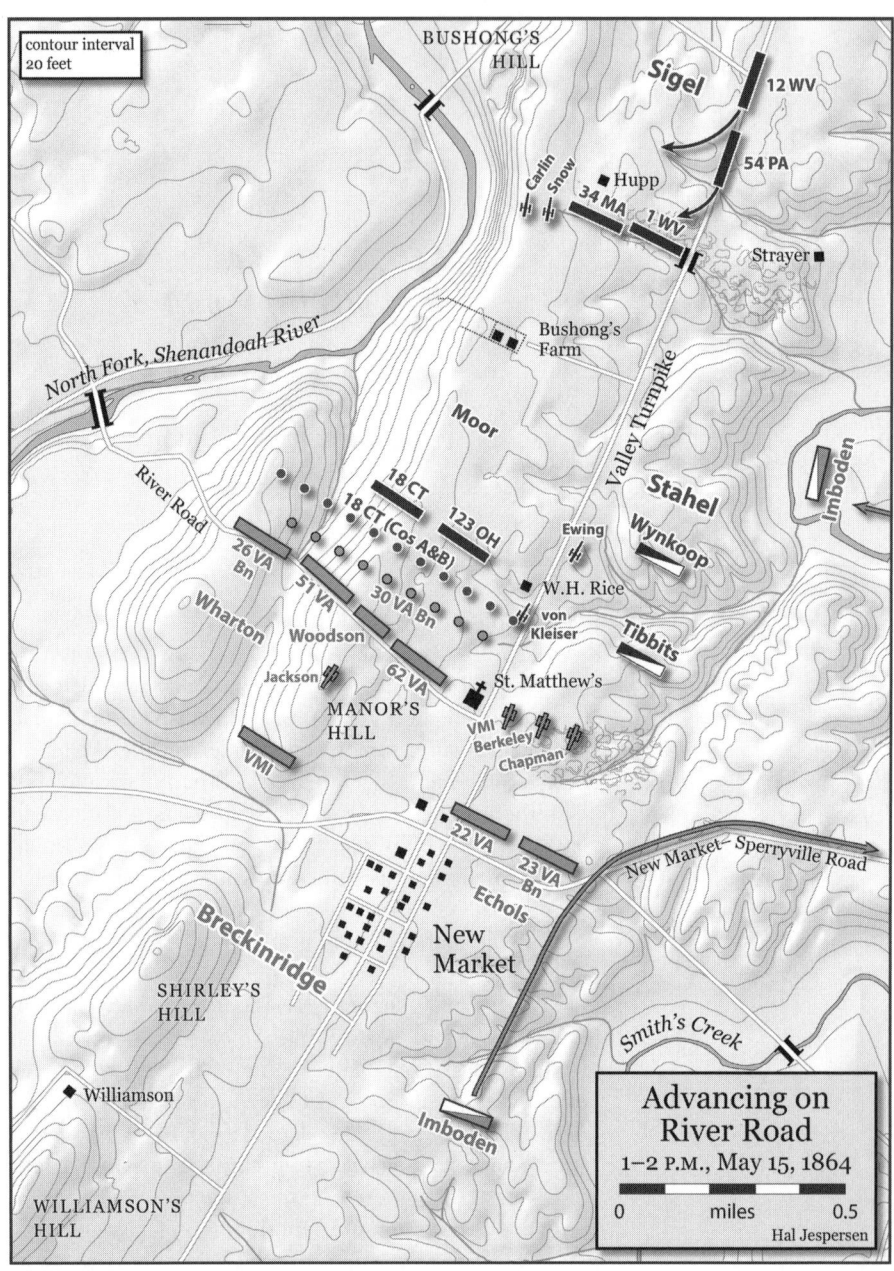

ADVANCING ON THE RIVER ROAD—Colonel Moor tried to establish new defensive lines along River Road, but the Confederates pressed forward with an unstoppable momentum, forcing the Union soldiers to fall back to new lines.

Before the Union troops had settled in this second battle position, "the rebels heralded their advance by their peculiar yell, and advanced in two strong lines, by far overlapping our own. Our skirmishers were driven in, and after a short but resolute struggle this line was

forced to the rear, which created some confusion in the Eighteenth Connecticut Regiment."

Echol's rebels had advanced through town and now poised on the Ohioan flank about the same time Wharton's men hit the Connecticut boys. Edmund P. Snyder remembered the moment the Confederates pushed forward on the new position, writing, "they pour in upon us such a storm of shot and shell so thick that the very air seemed alive with bullets."

Meanwhile, Von Kleiser wisely decided to remove his six cannon from the churchyard and redeploy on the Valley Pike, where the roadbed would ideally not mire his guns beyond rescue. The artillery captain hoped the infantry and Wynkoop's or Tibbits's cavalry could screen and shield his withdrawal. However, the Confederate gunners spotted Von Kleiser's intended movement and concentrated their fire toward his position, damaging one cannon by knocking off its wheel. Determined, the Union gunners lashed the horses and managed to drag the broken cannon down the Valley Pike. Losing a gun required military explanations, and with the difficulties of the day, the battery commander needed to avoid attracting negative attention to himself and his men. The battered cannon scraped down the road with its steel undercarriage creating sparks as it hit road rocks.

However, the cannon then "mired down and the

The church in the background of this photo stands on the location of St. Matthew's Lutheran Church at the time of the battle; however, the current structure is not the one from 1864. In St. Matthew's Cemetery, Von Kleiser's battery unlimbered and fired at the Confederates on Shirley's Hill. When the Confederates advanced on Moor's second defensive line, the artillery captain tried to haul his guns out of this position and farther down the Valley Pike, eventually going into position near the center of the Union line on Bushong's Hill. (skb)

Col. Augustus Moor had been the senior commander for the Union on the field at New Market until Gen. Stahel and later Gen. Sigel arrived; his first defensive lines faced the Confederates through the morning and were accepted by his superiors. Unfortunately, the Confederate advances frustrated his plans and forced several retreats and the establishment of new lines during the day. (fag)

horses couldn't pull it and they unhitched the horses and left it," Abe Park, a soldier in the 123rd Ohio, vividly remembered. Von Kleiser removed five cannon, leaving behind the damaged gun and explaining that the gun carriage had jammed with large road rocks, making it impossible to move, especially with gray-clad howlers heading down the pike.

Sigel and his officers started establishing a new position on Bushong's Hill, just north of Jacob Bushong's house and barn. Tired regiments from Thoburn's brigade had plodded quickly to the field and taken defensive positions. The 34th Massachusetts, 54th Pennsylvania, 1st West Virginia, and 12th West Virginia filtered into this new line. Communication crumbled along with Moor's River Road line. As the afternoon wore on, "Sigel seemed in a state of excitement and rode here and there with Stahel and Moor, all jabbering in German. In his excitement he seemed to forget his English entirely, and the purely American portion of his staff were totally useless to him."

Colonel Moor tried to salvage the situation, but found a continuously confusing scene. "I was ordered to bring up the two other regiments of my brigade to the support of a battery on the left in the rear, forming a third line," he reported. "After some inquiry where these regiments could be found, I learned that five companies of the Twenty-eighth and the One hundred and sixteenth Regiments Ohio Volunteer Infantry, under the command of Colonel Washburn, were in charge of the [supply] train, and did not leave Woodstock until 8 a.m. They had been halted at Mount Jackson, six miles in our rear. I sent my staff officers to order them up double-quick." Clearly, Sigel had forgotten the locations of his units or failed to remember the distances they had to march. To Moor, it might have felt like grasping for straws. The colonel could not prevent the collapse of his second line, but at least another defensive position was forming along Bushong's Hill.

Moor's regiments were not the only units "missing" or delayed near Mount Jackson. General Sullivan had infantry and artillery units making a leisurely march up the valley. Capt. Henry A. DuPont, commander of Battery B, 5th U.S. Artillery, gave a glimpse into this scene in the rear:

On the morning of the 15th of May, this Division [Sullivan's], which was marching southward on the valley turnpike, made a short halt about noon, some three or four miles from the battlefield [near Rude's Hill], to give the men an opportunity to eat and rest, no one having any idea that a battle was immediately imminent. As the weather was very warm, as soon as the halt was ordered I asked and received General Sullivan's personal permission to unhitch and water the horses of my Battery at a little stream…which was some 600 yards to the right, or east, of the turnpike. While the horses were drinking, an unexpected order came from General Sigel to send forward two batteries as rapidly as possible, and General Sullivan informed me that as my horses were not hitched up and several hundred yards from the pieces, he would order forward the other batteries…to save any loss of time. Soon afterwards, a second order arrived directing him to move at once with his Infantry, and, to my surprise, he interpreted this order literally and told me I would have to remain where I was, but that he would send for me as soon as he reached the front. . . .

Cpt. Henry DuPont—a West Point graduate—eventually brought his artillery battery up to the battle area, but his commanding officer did not feel the need to rush more guns to the scene. Ultimately, DuPont's delayed arrival would provide providential support for the Union troops at the end of the day. (nps)

Timing is difficult to determine with accuracy at the battle of New Market. Officers and soldiers provided different memories of certain times and, since the day was overcast and rainy, even observations on the day's lighting are not much help to researchers. It seems DuPont's timing might be a little quick, since around noon they should have heard cannon fire from New Market unless an acoustical shadow interfered. However, perhaps Sullivan arrived at Rude's Hill in the time between the collapse of Moor's second line and the beginning of the fight on the Bushong lines when the artillery pieces were maneuvering into new positions.

Ultimately, the more important glimpse of history in DuPont's account was the lack of hurry, lack of communication, and Sullivan's lack of initiative. The general seemed to lack enthusiasm in this campaign and battle, and considering his personal history, it might not be difficult to surmise some causes. First, Sullivan, a "left-over general," stayed in Sigel's command by default. Second, he may not have been delighted when the German-American general replaced his father-in-law in command of the Department of West Virginia. Third, Sullivan's nationality likely precluded him from invitations to Sigel's inner clique of German friends. By May 15, Sullivan, who had experience fighting in the Shenandoah Valley, may have felt stuck between the proverbial "rock and a hard place." Perhaps to survive

Strangely, Jeremiah Sullivan did not hurry troops to Sigel at New Market, spending most of the day in the Mount Jackson and Rude's Hill area. Questions still remain about his lack of action. (loc)

Looking north toward the Union defensive position along River Road. The line of trees along the rise visible in the distance at the right marks the position, which stretched east to St. Matthew's Church. Today, the modern interstate cuts through the battlefield, and a little imagination is required to visualize how it might have looked in 1864. (skb)

and avoid irritating his commander, Sullivan opted to follow the new orders literally. Given Sigel's recent outbursts that very morning, his strange penchant for war games, and the unlikely tactics he employed throughout the campaign, Sullivan may have been trying to survive and avoid a confrontation.

While Sigel struggled with leadership, Breckinridge performed well, stretching his infantry into one long battle line. From town and the Valley Pike to the crest of the river bank on Manor's Hill, the Confederate line prepared to literally sweep the field. Meanwhile, the artillerymen in gray limbered up and shifted their guns to new positions to keep firing on the Yankees. The battle line moved northward across the plateau between Manor's Hill toward the Bushong Farm, encountering the dead and wounded from the abandoned Union position. Breckinridge and his staff moved around the battlefield, directing and taking in the moment of forward triumph as the sky darkened, promising a storm.

General Imboden and the cavalry still covered the Confederate right flank, keeping a close eye on Stahel's horsemen while waiting in the trees and avoiding heavy losses. The Virginian believed he had discovered a brilliant opportunity for his cavalry, and when Breckinridge agreed to the new plan, Imboden prepared to move his horsemen and four artillery pieces from McClanahan's Battery across the rain-swollen Smith's Creek. Ideally, this would extend the Confederate right flank, covering New Market Gap and giving an opportunity to fire on the Union's flank, or head north to cut off Sigel's retreat route.

As for Colonel Moor and his regiments, the infantry pulled back on orders from Colonel Kellog of the 123rd Ohio. The 18th Connecticut tried to wriggle around the barn, outhouses, and fenced-in farm lane by marching "by the flank at the double quick." The farm lane ended farther than anticipated and the regiment fell into confusion before rallying and reforming in the rear of the new troops on the Bushong line. One of the things James Haggerty from Connecticut remembered from the first half of the battle was his regiment's colorbearer. "As I looked at Jim's bronzed face as he stood holding the colors I saw no sign of fear," he said, "instead he waved the flag, signal fashion at the advancing Confederates."

Moor's second line had broken, but Union defenders still had their patriotic spirit. The battle was far from over, and the boys in blue prepared to meet the Confederates in a new position and with counterattacks.

Part of River Road east of the interstate was acquired in 2018 by the Shenandoah Valley Battlefields Foundation and will be preserved for study and battle interpretation. Check with SVBF or New Market Battlefield State Historical Site to see if the property is open for a visit since there are still residents on the tract. (skb)

On Manor's Hill

This area is where the 18th Connecticut and 123rd Ohio held skirmish lines on Manor's Hill and watched the first advance of the Confederates down Shirley's Hill. Try to imagine spending a rainy night here and waking to watch gathering enemy troops with the sinking feeling that your own reinforcements were miles away.

Here, James Haggerty remembered, "As they [Confederates] emerged from the woods and descended the hill, my attention was attracted to a tall fellow who took no advantage of shells, but came forward. His big gray hat was pushed back on his head. He was in advance of any other skirmisher. I raised my rifle and took deliberate aim at him, but for some reason or other I did not fire. I believe every other man on the line fired at him. The last I saw of him surrounded by battle smoke he was making a break for our line. . . ."

➤ ON THE WAY TO STOP 10

Exit the hotel and house of worship driveway. Turn left and in about 0.3 miles, as an optional stop before Stop 10, use the pullout on the left to see the terrain of Manor's Hill and the plateau. As you drive, note the private museum on your left. This structure basically sits at the location of River Road and St. Matthews is directly east; this is approximately where Moor's second line fought.

GPS for the pullout: 38.655153 N, -78.672563 W

If you exit your vehicle at the pull out, notice how the land is significantly flatter here after the hills to the south. When Confederate troops reached this point in the battle, Breckinridge's infantry was basically one sweeping forward line with the reserves following a safe distance behind. This impressive formation continued until the eastern part of the line hit the Bloody Cedars near the Valley Pike and the western line encountered the Bushong Farm. Still together, the line halted and came into the battle positions explained in the next chapters.

Exit the pullout and go left, continuing about 0.4 miles to the entrance to the Virginia Museum of the Civil War and New Market Battlefield State Historical Park (Stop 1). You will enter large gates and make a sweeping turn to see the drum-shaped museum. Park and enter the visitor center to purchase a pass to explore this area of the preserved battlefield.

GPS for the Virginia Museum of the Civil War:
57 George Collins Pkwy, New Market, VA 22844
38.662619 N, -78.670630 W

At the Virginia Museum of the Civil War

You'll continue the next few tour stops on foot. Please be certain to purchase a battlefield pass and note the closing times of the Virginia Museum of the Civil War and New Market Battlefield State Historical Park. The parking lot and gate/tunnel to the 54th Pennsylvania Monument close promptly at the posted times. You can visit the Pennsylvania statue from Route 11 if you do not have time or inclination to walk under the highway and into the Bloody Cedars.

Be sure to plan time to explore the Virginia Museum of the Civil War. Cadet uniforms, pieces of the VMI battle flag, weapons, original art, a Bushong family quilt, and other impressive artifacts are on display. If you have time, view the documentary film in the museum theater and pick up a battlefield tour pamphlet. The book tour will guide you along a similar route with a few exceptions and additional notes, but you may enjoy reading the battlefield paper and noting the numbered posts and extra history along the way.

Top: The main exhibit hall at the Virginia Museum of the Civil War features displays of New Market artifacts and other objects of Civil War interest. (skb)

Above: The beautiful stained glass mural in the Virginia Museum of the Civil War offers artistic interpretation of the history and battle. Perhaps the Shenandoah River is suggested by the flowing lines. Be sure to notice the official seals worked into the glass and the list of fallen cadets' names. (skb)

⟶ **To Stop 10**

If you intend to walk the battlefield, follow the cut/marked trail from the museum toward the Bushong House. (Alternately, you can drive to the Bushong House. Pull-off parking is to the right, directly across from the house.)

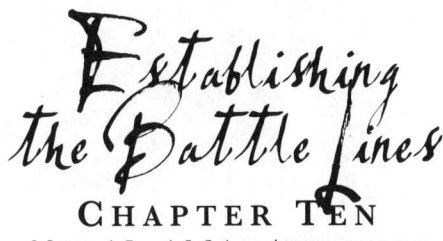

Establishing the Battle Lines

CHAPTER TEN

MAY 15, 1864—AFTERNOON

"We marched three days and nights, through rain and storms, without a wink of sleep and hardly a morsel to eat during that time . . . halting at Mount Jackson a moment we heard heavy cannonading in advance a few miles," Union Dr. Alexander Neil explained to his family in a letter penned less than a week after the battle of New Market. "We soon learned that Longstreet, Breckinridge, and Imboden were fighting our force in advance at New Market some 5 miles distant, so we were ordered up by Sigel on double quick, the rain pouring down in torrents the whole time. . . ." Curiously, the doctor believed the rumor that the Confederates had significantly more troops than they did, as well as an inflated report about the rebel leadership.

"When we came up all exhausted and drenched with rain to the skin," he continued, "the cannons were belching forth their music like the crashing of a thousand thunders . . . the heavens were literally blackened with shells and canister. My Brigade rushed up to the slaughter pen, and there the volleys of musketry opened out on both sides."

Surgeons like Dr. Neil would display as much courage as the soldiers and officers during the battle, rushing onto the field to rescue the injured from the mire, setting up dressing stations in the torrential downpour, and commandeering structures to perform surgeries.

Neil's regiment—the 12th West Virginia—served in Col. Joseph Thoburn's brigade and arrived in time to take a position on the Union's new line along Bushong's

Union and Confederate troops ran past the Bushong farm, rushing to establish new battle lines. Caught in the middle, the family became bystanders and participants in the historic battle, and their home still stands as a monument to their actions and courage. (skb)

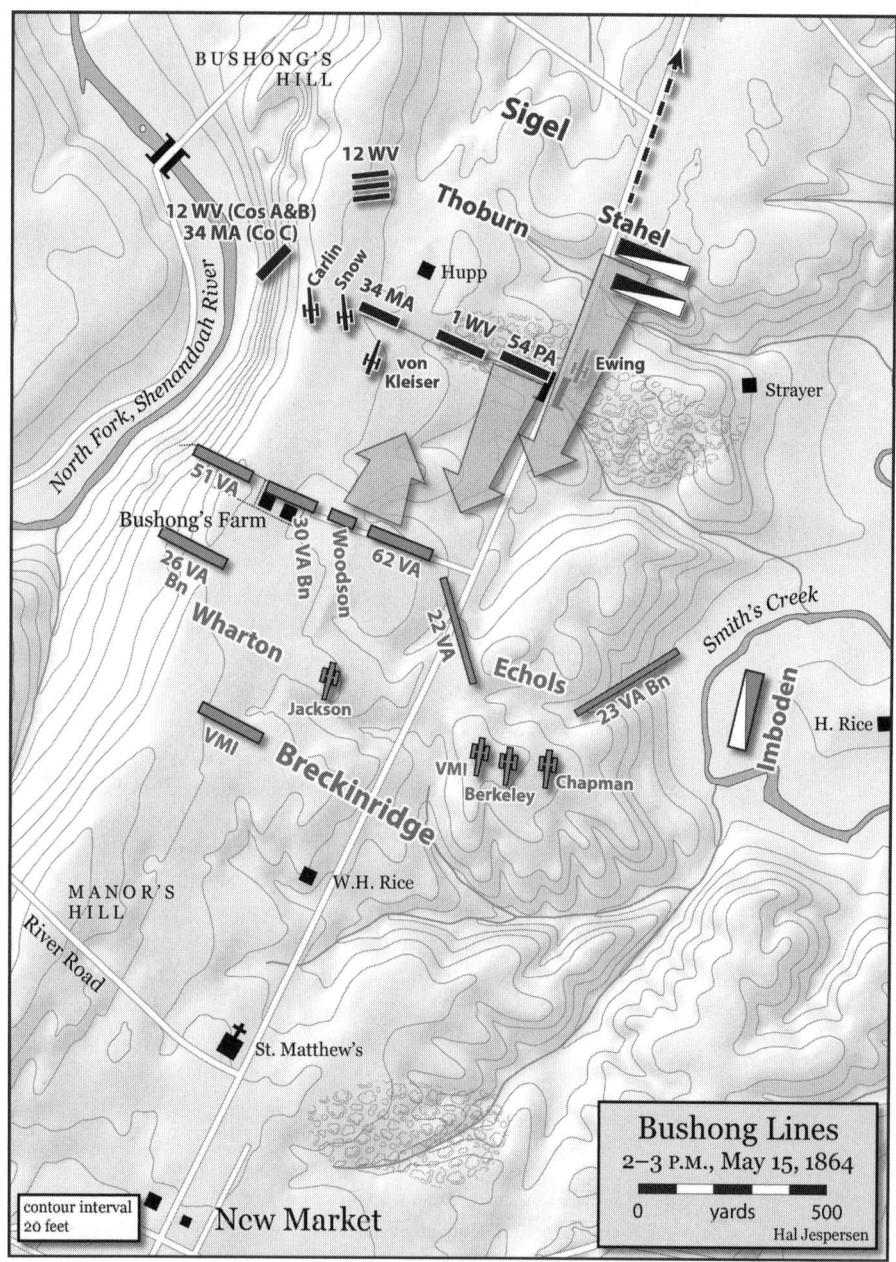

Bushong Lines
2–3 P.M., May 15, 1864

0   yards   500

Hal Jespersen

contour interval
20 feet

Bushong Lines—Near the Bushong farm, Union and Confederate lines stretched west to east, positioning on either side of open fields and a small ravine. The Shenandoah River and Smith Creek created restrictive borders, keeping the fighting in lines along the rises and preventing any large-scale flanking maneuvers.

Hill, commanding open fields. Sigel spent most of his afternoon personally placing artillery on the new line and managed to develop what would have been an impressive, impromptu position—had it been a dry day.

Jacob Bushong's farm sat between and at the center of the new Union and Confederate lines. North of the farm and orchard, Bushong's Hill rises above a lower field—then planted and likely flooded—and connects to the high river bluff just to the west. The rise of ground stretches east, losing elevation as it runs into the Valley Pike. Along this rise, hill, and bluff, Sigel established the Union's third defensive line at New Market, filtering in the regiments arriving from the march.

Carlin's and Snow's batteries positioned themselves on the river's high bluff, commanding an artillery sweep over the open field toward the Bushong house and orchard and farther south, down toward the cedars. To the artillery's left, the 34th Massachusetts waited, standing in an open field with no significant protection. The 1st West Virginia sandwiched themselves between the Bay State boys and the 54th Pennsylvania; the latter regiment completed the line to the Valley Pike, where Ewing's guns and Stahel's cavalry finished the flank defense. The 12th West Virginia hung back behind Snow's and Carlin's guns and the 34th Massachusetts; depending on their exact position, they may have been somewhat sheltered by the curvature of the hill, especially if they had crouched or laid low. Moor's regiments from the earlier fight tried to regroup behind Thoburn's brigade and line while Von Kleiser placed his five remaining cannon basically in front of the Massachusett's regiment in a semi-advanced position: the rise of Bushong's Hill above the soggy field.

As for Breckinridge's line, his main infantry advance remained basically similar, still moving ahead in one battle line with the reserves forming a second line

On a clear day, Sigel could have seen his entire line from Bushong's Hill and even enjoyed this picturesque view of New Market Gap. Notice the trees in the distance in the left of the photo; beyond the modern highway and in that area, the 54th Pennsylvania anchored the line on the Valley Pike with cavalry on the flank. To the right, the Bushong farm is visible, marking the area of the Confederate line. (skb)

A cut trail, also marked with numbered posts that correspond to the state park's tour guide, runs from the museum toward the Bushong farm. These are the footsteps of the Confederate troops, and later the VMI Cadets, as they headed toward the fences and new battle lines just beyond the farm structures. (skb)

farther back. On the Confederate left flank—along the river bluff—Wharton's Brigade moved ahead. The 51st Virginia was closest to the river, then the 30th Virginia Battalion, Woodson's Missourians, and the 62nd Virginia, which anchored on the Valley Pike. Following Wharton's Brigade, the 26th Virginia Battalion had been forced behind the 51st by the curving river bluffs. The Virginia Military Institute Cadets hung back on the plateau as the forward brigade moved into position. The infantrymen rushed past the Bushong House and into line along the north orchard fence and slight rise of ground that stretched through Strayer's pasture field with sporadically growing cedars toward the pike. Behind this infantry line, Jackson's four guns were unlimbered. Across the Valley Pike from the 62nd Virginia and on a perfect rise of ground, the VMI artillery and Berkeley's and Chapman's batteries rolled into position. Echol's brigade with the 22nd Virginia Infantry and 23rd Virginia Infantry supported those guns on the east side of the pike.

Smith Creek, the wandering, twisting branch, turned close to the new battle lines. Its flooded waters created a natural barrier to the east and allowed Imboden and McClanahan's battery to approach close to Stahel's cavalry. To the west, the Shenandoah River also made a sweeping turn inward at this point of the battlefield, crafting an almost hourglass type of funnel where the

armies would fight. With Smith Creek and the high river bluffs, extreme flanking maneuvers would be difficult for either side, leaving two options: retreat to different ground or issue commands for a slug-fest, artillery duel, or deadly charges into the open fields separating the two armies.

    The battle moved fluidly, without an organized "time out" to prepare these battle lines. The troops on both sides reached these positions and continued the fight. Colonel George D. Wells, commander of the 34th Massachusetts Infantry, described the situation:

Jackson's Confederate artillery pieces positioned south and slightly east of the Bushong's house, firing on the Union line and dueling with the Yankee cannon. A single artillery piece marks their place on the battlefield today. (skb)

> *In front was rolling ground. . . . The rebels advanced in . . . lines of battle . . . with masses on the right and left. The ground was perfectly open, not a tree or shrub to obstruct the view. Nothing could be finer than their advance. Their yelling grew steadily nearer; our skirmishers and infantry in front came back on the double-quick, some of them running through and over my lines.*

> *The air was filled with bullets and bursting shells, and my men began to fall. I was ordered to deploy one company across my front as skirmishers, and Captain Leach, with Company G, went forward, and his groups halted and deployed in the tumult about 200 yards in advance, each man taking his exact interval and dressing*

to the right as steadily as on drill. The officers in the line were giving their orders in low tones, and every man stood, his gun at the ready, his finger on the trigger, waiting to see the face of his foe. It was a marvel to me then and is now how men who almost never before had heard the rebel yell and the terrible din of the battle-field could be so entirely calm and self-possessed. Soon our men in front were, by the confusion, cleared away, the rebel lines were plainly seen, and the battle began.

Dr. Neil from the 12th West Virginia had an advantaged though dangerous view of the field from his horse. He also noted continued determination as the Confederates reached the Bushong line. "[T]he noise so terrible and the scene so frightful," he said, "the rebels advancing on us like a stone wall, never flinching for a moment, though their ranks were thinned every moment and the ground was covered with their dead and wounded. I never saw braver men than those rebels, they fight worthier of a nobler cause."

East of the Bushong House and beyond the modern-day highway, this line of trees and trail marks part of the Confederate line along the southside of Strayer's Pasture. In this area and a little advanced, the 62nd Virginia fired on the 54th Pennsylvania. (skb)

The casualties of the day's previous combat and the continual cries of hurting men signaled the need for skilled surgeons. Sigel's medical director met Dr. Neil as he arrived on the battlefield and "ordered me to proceed immediately upon the field and see to the wounded, getting them in the ambulances." Neil obeyed and risked his own life to oversee the rescue and removal of the wounded, finding himself "where the minnie balls and canister were flying like hail and fairly strewing the ground with dead and wounded."

For some regiments, the battle had just begun. For others, the day of shot and shell continued. Still others found themselves fighting to survive horrific and painful injuries. Crushed, pierced, broken, bleeding, trampled— the casualties of war staggered off the field or collapsed in the mud. Whether their jackets were blue, butternut, or cadet gray, they cried, bled, and died as victims of the inhumanity of war.

And the worst fighting of the day was yet to come.

At the Bushong House

As you walk across the cut/marked trail toward the Bushong House from the museum, you are following the route Wharton's brigade would have taken at this point in the battle. If the historic home is open for visitors, explore the rooms and displays. Peer into the workshops and barn, if you like, and think about the Bushongs' experiences as they hid in their cellar, peering out those basement windows and seeing rushing feet hurrying past their house and to the new battle lines. Return to the Bushong House for the next chapter's walking directions.

➤ TO STOPS 11-14

To continue the walking tour, stand at the Bushong House and face east (toward New Market Gap and Highway 81). You should see a tunnel passage under the highway. Walk through—noting the gate closing time to ensure you'll have enough exploration time. As you emerge from the tunnel, you enter the area now called "Bloody Cedars," which was called Strayer's Pasture during the Civil War. Follow the battlefield trail into the low ravine.

NOTE: If you intend to drive to the 54th Pennsylvania Monument instead of walking, continue to the next chapter's tour notes and restart the tour at the Missouri marker, which is located north of the Bushong House and yard fences beside the paved road. If you drive to the tour stop in Chapter 16, refer back to these notes for cavalry charge details to see in the topography.

GPS for Tunnel Passage Entrance: 38.663129 N, -78.666934 W.

During the battle, the Bushong family hid in their cellar. This door is one of the entrances to the underground room. Interestingly, their cellar is not completely below ground level, and windows offered a glimpse of hurrying boots or falling soldiers along with danger from stray projectiles on May 15, 1864. (skb)

This tunnel runs underneath the highway, allowing visitors to walk safely to the eastern side of the battlefield to explore the cavalry area and the Bloody Cedars. (skb)

Of Mud and Hoofbeats

CHAPTER ELEVEN

MAY 15, 1864—MID-AFTERNOON

Jacob Lester, a horseman in the 1st New York Veteran Cavalry, had thus far seen little action on this battle day. Drenching wet, he and his comrades and their horses had been held in reserve positions and collected by General Stahel, who seemed to have a penchant for gathering regiments from their rightful commanders and holding the units under his own eye. "It was raining hard for the last hour," Lester wrote, "the ground was soaked, we were on low ground and there were puddles of water everywhere about us."

While the Confederates pressed their attack and halted along the Bushong lines, perhaps Lester wished for coffee and a stable for his horse. Perhaps he was grateful that he had not been called into serious combat. That changed as the 62nd Virginia and Echol's men advanced close enough to fire on the massed Union cavalry while, somewhere on the east side of Smith Creek, Imboden and a few cannon lurked, waiting for a chance to harass their opponents. The 1st New York and other units started taking casualties.

Stahel decided the cavalry had been inactive enough for one day and concocted a grand scheme fit for a Napoleonic battlefield, but which would not translate well on the Valley Pike. Lester remembered the orders this way: "the worst was yet to come. We got orders to 'draw sabre' and I knew we were to charge the oncoming line of rebel infantry."

The route for the intended cavalry charge ran directly along the pike, which at this spot had been

From the Confederate line and approximate high ground position of the 62nd Virginia, this overlook of the Valley Pike shows how the land where the cavalry charged might have looked on a clear day. (skb)

Julius Stahel—one of Sigel's immigrant officers—attempted to employ Napoleonic style cavalry tactics at New Market. A combination of poor visibility, rough terrain, mud, and the fire power from Confederate artillery defeated his efforts. (loc)

Collier Minge commanded the VMI Cadet artillery section during the battle of New Market. Still a cadet himself, he handled the guns well, following orders and playing a role in stopping the cavalry charge. (vmi)

neatly bordered by low stone walls. To make matters worse, the road descended into the shallow ravine that ran from the Bushongs' down through the cedar pasture. The Valley Pike was stone based, but the amount of rain over the last few days still created a frightful amount of mud for the cavalry to pass through before ascending the opposite slope, where the Confederate infantry and artillery moved into position. For the cavalrymen advancing on the unpaved ground, the mud was even deeper.

Could a smashing cavalry charge stop and outflank the Confederate line? Stahel must have thought such a chance exsited.

Despite the battle smoke and rain, Breckinridge spotted or heard the assembling cavalry and suspected their plans. According to his aide, the general directed the recently arrived artillerymen to add double shot canister to their guns. Cadet Collier Minge, commander of the VMI artillery section, admitted, "We got quickly into action with canister against cavalry charging down the road and adjacent fields. . . ." The Confederate infantry also maneuvered to receive the coming cavalry charge. The 62nd Virginia and 22nd Virginia refused their lines slightly, creating an angle running back to the Confederate batteries, which dominated the road and low ground. The 23rd Virginia moved to the east side of the cannons, creating another side of a defensive "V."

Rand Noyes of the 22nd Virginia Infantry remembered the moment of Stahel's charge:

> [T]he enemies' Cavalry attempted a charge (Column Closed 'en masse.') One of our shells bursted in the head of their column killing many horses & men directly on the stone bridge over the ravine crossing the Pike and about 200 yards in front of the 22nd Va's right. Only one man on an unmanageable horse came through on the Pike & between 22nd VA. . . . Almost immediately following this charge of the enemies cavalry the 22nd started a charge on the enemy in their front and their [rout] began. . . .

One noncommissioned officer from the 1st Maryland Potomac Home Brigade summed it up simply: "They were ready for us." Decimated by the hastily placed artillery and quick-moving infantry, the Union cavalry suffered most of its casualties of the entire campaign in Stahel's ill-fated cavalry charge.

What had prompted Stahel to think this charge

A modern view of the Confederate gun placements to counter the Union cavalry charge. Breckinridge probably did not have this type of visibility but prepared for the attack he thought, knew, or saw was coming up the turnpike. (skb)

was a good idea? It employed classic European cavalry tactics—generally suicidal during the Crimean War and American Civil War—which the Hungarian would have studied in the Old World. Could the charge have worked if the Confederate artillery had not been there? Could the blue-clad horseman have actually turned the Southern right flank? Maybe. Just maybe—on a good day. However, to order approximately one thousand cavalry down a comparatively narrow muddy pike and swampy roadside seems lacking in sound judgment. In Stahel's defense, he probably could not have seen the artillery moving into position during heavy rain, especially if battle smoke also hung in the wet air. Either way, Gen. Stahel's risk analysis failed to consider the topography and weather; his men and horses paid the price. After the grand charge into the ravine of death, the Union cavalry fell back and assumed only guard duties; later, they would help cover the Union retreat.

As for the Confederate cavalry, Imboden and his troopers had been absent from the area of the main fighting. With Breckinridge's permission, they had

Brigadier General John Imboden had performed successful cavalry operations and had even been tasked with guarding the Confederate ambulance train during the retreat from Gettysburg in 1863, but at New Market a flooded creek prevented him from taking a major role in the fighting on May 15. (wc)

crossed swollen Smith's Creek to take position on the Union's flank. The creek between them created a natural barrier and, with McClanahan's guns, Imboden sent an enfilading fire into the Union forces during the retreat to the Bushong line.

The Rebel cavalry leader probably crossed the creek with another objective. If he crossed Smith Creek one more time, farther north, he would be in Sigel's rear and within striking distance of the single bridge over the Shenandoah River at Mount Jackson. Destroy that bridge and, if Breckinridge just pushed Sigel into a retreat, the Union escape would be cut off.

Surprisingly, Imboden's activity diminished as the battle day wore on. He did not take any particularly noted action to repulse Stahel's charge, though he could have been within artillery range. Nor did the Confederate cavalry return to the west of the creek and rejoin the army at any time during the fight. The question has haunted battle studies: why? It seems unlikely Imboden got lost or suffered a case of cowardice. Most likely Smith Creek was the culprit. Though normally low and placid, the massive amounts of rain had turned the branch into a swift-moving, deep torrent. It is quite possible Imboden and his horsemen crossed at the bridge near the foot of Massanutten Mountain and, by the time they prepared to cross farther north or at the bridge, the water had risen higher. As an experienced horseman, Imboden must have realized the extreme danger of forcing the horses to swim or cross a wobbling bridge under the circumstances. Whatever the reason, Imboden and the Confederate cavalry did not return en masse and failed to take part in the end of the day's fight.

Smith Creek—looking relatively calm in this photo—threatened cavalrymen during the battle with its flooded, rushing water and created a natural barrier that prevented effective Confederate cavalry operations. This photo of the creek was taken at one of the fords on a modern country road. After exploring this area, it's easier to understand how the swift-rising waters could have trapped Imboden and his cavalry. (skb)

Artillery, infantry, rain, and maybe a swollen creek effectively knocked the Union and Confederate cavalries out of the battle. While Stahel's cavalry made their headlong charge into disaster and Imboden delayed on the far side of Smith's Creek, the two infantries continued their battle along the Bushong lines. In the midst of that cacophony of battle at New Market, the sound of thundering cavalry had been permanently replaced by the tired clop of weary hooves in puddles and mud and the screams of dying horses, kicking in the battlefield filth alongside their fallen masters who had once dreamed of gloriously heroic cavalry charges.

Along the Pike and at the Bloody Cedars

Route 11 is on the roadbed of the Old Valley Turnpike. Walk to a rise where you can clearly see the road. Notice the low dip even in the modern road. This is the ground and road where Stahel sent his cavalrymen, moving left to right from your current position.

Spot the hotel on the ridge to the right? That is basically where Breckinridge massed his artillery in the rainstorm to receive the coming charge.

Look beyond Route 11. The dense trees mark the location of Smith's Creek. Notice how close it is to the battlefield, pressing in as a natural barrier on man's fight.

Continue to the 54th Pennsylvania Regiment Monument located to the north.

GPS for the 54th Pennsylvania Regiment Monument
38.665464 N, -78.661939 W

The 54th Pennsylvania monument is visible in the distance from the Confederate artillery position along the Valley Pike. (skb)

"May God Forgive Me"

CHAPTER TWELVE

MAY 15, 1864—MID-AFTERNOON

"As soon as we arrived on that Ridge or Raise we began to fire," Sergeant Bryan of Company A of the 54th Pennsylvania recalled, "and I was kept busy pulling our men back out of the line as they were killed or wounded and the smoke was so thick I could see nothing in front as we lined up for battle and the 1st New York Cavalry broke through our line and put us in some confusion. . . ." This glimpse of battle exemplifies the situation in the infantry line near the turnpike immediately after Stahel's cavalry charge.

The battle of New Market unfolded as a moving battle. It proceeded comparatively simply with the Confederates advancing and the Union retreating. However, on the Bushong lines, a period of uncoordinated attacks and counterattacks occurred. Much of it was likely simultaneous or at least occurred with such an ebb and flow that it is challenging to declare with perfect certainty what happened first.

East of the Bushongs' fields, the soldiers also positioned themselves on either side of Strayer's pasture, a rocky area with rolling rises and low cedar trees. Battle smoke created a cocoon over the fields, isolating the rolling topography and preventing officers from seeing along their lines. The 54th Pennsylvania made an advance "on the extreme left of the line of battle," recounted its colonel, Jacob M. Campbell. "We remained in this position, partly shielded from the fire of the enemy by the crest of a hill in front, until, observing the regiment on my right making a charge in absence of

The 54th Pennsylvania Monument stands like a silent sentinel, overlooking the battle position of the regiment and keeping watch over the field where the men charged. (skb)

Many primary sources describing the fight in the pasture and the "Bloody Cedars" area mention a deep ravine running the length of the field toward the Valley Pike. Seen here, the ravine cuts through the battlefield and would have extended farther west in 1864; the modern-day highway interferes with the ravine's course closer to the Bushong house. (skb)

orders, presuming it proper to imitate their example, I ordered the Fifty-fourth also to charge, which was done with alacrity and spirit."

Plunging into the battle smoke without direct orders, Campbell's men soon encountered disaster. The pastureland dips into the small ravine that had caused trouble for the cavalry. As the regiment crested one of the rises, they came under direct fire from the 62nd Virginia—normally a cavalry unit but fighting dismounted this day. The Pennsylvanian and Rebel soldiers exchanged volleys.

G.W. Gageby's memories of the 54th Pennsylvania's advance shows the confusion on the field as regiments maneuvered almost independently. "I could hear cheering on our right front but the smoke was so dense I could not see anything in front. I moved over to the right and close up to Co A then noticed they were firing to the right oblique but could not see any troops in that direction." Gageby then moved forward on his own to "the north side of the stream of water running down the ravine, passing up a well-beaten path to a house near which. . . . I picked up a wounded man of the 34th Mass Inf and carried him onto the porch of the house. . . . Opened the nearest door intending to take him in. As the door swung open I saw through the window opposite it a line of Confederates passing along the other side of the house. I turned to go back to my Regt and saw them

This view, looking south over Strayer's Pasture, looks deceptively pleasant with softly rolling rises. However, the field is rocky with stony obstacles offering additional dangers to the charging Union soldiers. (skb)

falling back and to get back to them I would be between the fire of both parties." Gageby eventually scrambled back to his regiment, which was now in serious trouble.

The 22nd Virginia had moved and now enfiladed the Union regiment's left flank. With heavy fire from two sides and possible shots from the west side also, the Pennsylvania regiment had limited options. They could have refused their line, but circumstances dictated other action. "[M]y attention was called to the fact that the regiment on my right (owning to the overwhelming numbers brought against it) had given way, and the enemy was advancing at almost right angle with my line and extending beyond the rear and right of my regiment," Col. Campbell declared. "A few minutes only would be required to completely surround my regiment, and in the absence of any appearance of advancing support I was reluctantly compelled to order my command to retire."

Clearly, the situation farther west impacted the Pennsylvanian advance and retreat. There, the fighting had also been complex and tough.

On the Confederate line, between the 62nd Virginia and Wharton's 51st and 26th Virginia, Woodson's Missourians—formally called 1st Missouri, Company A—held their line and fought back.

The original sixty-two Missourians to arrive at New Market had experienced quite a journey to that battlefield. Missouri was a border state during the

Looking west and slightly north from the Confederates' line. Hidden by the smoke, storm, and gully, the boys in gray poured heavy fire into the advancing Pennsylvanians, halting their charge. (skb)

Civil War, and Missourians served on both sides. The men who formed Woodson's company had fought for the Confederacy in regiments and possibly guerrilla bands. They had all been captured— at Port Gibson, Vicksburg, and other locations. Held prisoner in Alton, Illinois, these Missourians had been exchanged in June 1863 at City Point, Virginia. Because travel back to Missouri would have been difficult and Virginia offered plenty of opportunity for fighting the Yankees, Charles H. Woodson persuaded the authorities in Richmond to allow him to organize the fellows from his state and stay to fight in the Old Dominion. He eventually got permission and, by August 1863, he had rallied about seventy men and become their captain. General John Imboden welcomed the little unit, which soon received the nickname "Missouri Exiles." Imboden had attached his new exiles to the footsore 62nd Virginia Cavalry, which fought dismounted because they lacked horses. In the early spring of 1864, Woodson's men officially re-enlisted with the Confederacy for "forty years or the war." These men planned to fight—win or lose.

Across from these "Missouri Exiles," Von Kleiser's battery of five cannon sent projectiles directly into their unit, blasting the Confederates along the orchard fence and lower pasture. There on the muddy battlefield,

"Woodson's heroes fell," far from their home state and often overshadowed by history, which is dominated by the Virginia story of the battle. Estimates of the Missourians' losses vary widely, from sixty-four to as a high as ninety percent; in either case, their losses represented the highest casualty rate at the battle of New Market.

Near the Missourians, another small unit likely fought. Company E of the 3rd Confederate Engineers— often called Hart's Engineers— had joined Breckinridge earlier in the campaign from McCausland's brigade. They began the battle with approximately forty-four men, equipped to fight as infantry, and seem to have moved locations on the battle line as the fight unfolded.

The Virginia regiments were in trouble. The 51st Virginia experienced some confusion crossing a fence at the far west end of the line; also, they lacked maneuvering room, crushed between the river cliffs and the units behind and to their right. The 26th Virginia— after following the 51st as reserves for most of the day—eventually wriggled into line on the 51st's right. Under fire and with limited visibility, these two regiments did not really notice a development farther east.

This small monument was erected in 1905 by two Missouri veterans with the help of another local veteran and the Bushongs. The inscription reads, "This rustic pile—The simple tale will tell:—It marks the spot— Where Woodson's Heroes fell." (skb)

As Woodson's Missourians and the 62nd Virginia maneuvered to counter Union advances, "confusion and disorder" appeared on the "right of [Wharton's] brigade." As Robert E. Wolfe from the 51st Virginia explained, "This no doubt was caused by the untimely advance of the 62nd and Clarke's battalion." That Confederate advance met repulse, but a gap had opened in the Confederate line.

On the north side of the Bushong orchard, no Confederate troops held the line between Wharton and the Missourians. With the 26th Virginia Regiment already positioned on the line, Breckinridge and his staff lacked an experienced unit to send into the gap. Shifting men from the engaged regiments to cover it would be difficult and might make the line so thin that another Union attack might burst through.

One of Breckinridge's aides, Maj. Charles Semple, kept the general informed of the line's situation, worrying how quickly the Union commanders would discover the weakness. Semple believed the time had come to use the reserves—the Virginia Military Institute cadets who still waited near the plateau, unengaged in the fight.

Breckinridge hesitated and objected. He saw the cadets as boys, young and inexperienced. Perhaps their youthful appearances had reminded him of his own boy, Cabell, who had impulsively rushed to join the Confederacy in 1861 and who had recently returned to his father from a Union prison. Semple waited, checked the situation, and insisted the gap must be filled. The cadets were a trained military force. They could enter the battle and secure Breckinridge's line. "General, it is too late," the major declared after making another effort to condense the Confederate troops already on the field into the gap. "The Federals are right on us. If the cadets are ordered up we can close the gap."

Breckinridge responded. Some said his voice broke with emotion as he declared, "Put the boys in, and may God forgive me for the order."

At the Pennsylvania and Missouri Monuments

At the 54th Pennsylvania Regiment monument, face south and note the undulating ground you have crossed and can see from the rise. This is the area obscured by thick battle smoke while the regiment moved forward and fought. The Confederate line was basically along the ridge now planted with trees on the far side of the open ground, though some had moved farther into the field.

On the Confederate line, the men of the 62nd Virginia, Hart's Engineers, and the Missourians stretched from this area, over the ground now blocked by the highway, and to approximately the corner of the Bushong fence where the Woodson Monument now stands.

Walk across the pasture in the

Veterans from the 54th Pennsylvania Regiment erected this monument on the New Market battlefield in October 1905, creating one of the few monuments to Pennsylvania troops within the state of Virginia. The inscription reads, "Erected to the memory of the heroic men of the 54th Regt. Pa. Vet. Vol. Inf. Who gave their lives in defence of their country." (skb)

The veterans called Strayer's pasture "the Bloody Cedars." In later years when they returned to New Market for the monument dedication, they dug up some sapling cedars and planted them in their cemeteries in the north to create a living memorial from this battlefield. (skb)

Pennsylvanians' footsteps and return to the main state park battlefield area via the tunnel. You should now be facing the Bushong House. Walk to the right along the road. Just beyond the orchard stands the Woodson memorial marker and an information sign.

GPS for Missouri Marker: 38.664047 N, -78.667144 W

From the Missouri Marker, walk west toward the river, following the rail fence. Notice the Bushong orchard and house to the left in a view that the soldiers could have seen if the smoke and rain were not too heavy.

Desperate Fighting
CHAPTER THIRTEEN
MAY 15, 1864—MID-AFTERNOON

Breckinridge's orders arrived for the cadets, who waited in relative safety on the plateau in the rear of the battle lines. Lieutenant Colonel Shipp and the cadet officers ordered the boys forward. As they advanced from the plateau and started down the incline toward the Bushong Farm, "we were subjected to a terrible fire of artillery," said one of the cadets. "When within four hundred yards of their (the Federal) line, three of our boys fell dead from the explosion of one shell, Cabell, Jones, and Crockett."

Again, the corps closed ranks and moved forward. Reaching the Bushong House, two companies rushed to the right of the building while the others moved to the left. Yards ahead, the rail fence waited as a place to mark and reform their line. More and more boys collapsed with wounds. Cadet McDowell from North Carolina fell, a bullet piercing his chest and killing him almost instantly. Cadet Evans rushed on with the flag—a white banner emblazoned with the Virginia seal; in his enthusiasm, the flag caught in a tree and several boys helped him disentangle it.

Near the Bushong property, Cadet Samuel Atwill received a painful wound in his leg and collapsed on the ground. Cadet Thomas Garland Jefferson—great-nephew of Founding Father Thomas Jefferson—paused to bind James Darden's gushing wound, tourniqueting his arm with a canteen strap. A few paces farther, a bullet slammed into seventeen-year-old Jefferson's chest, creating an agonizing wound.

Carlin's and Snow's batteries on Bushong's Hill dueled with Jackson's guns and swept the open fields, but their position was threatened by Wharton's advancing Confederates, who eventually took the hill and at least one cannon. (skb)

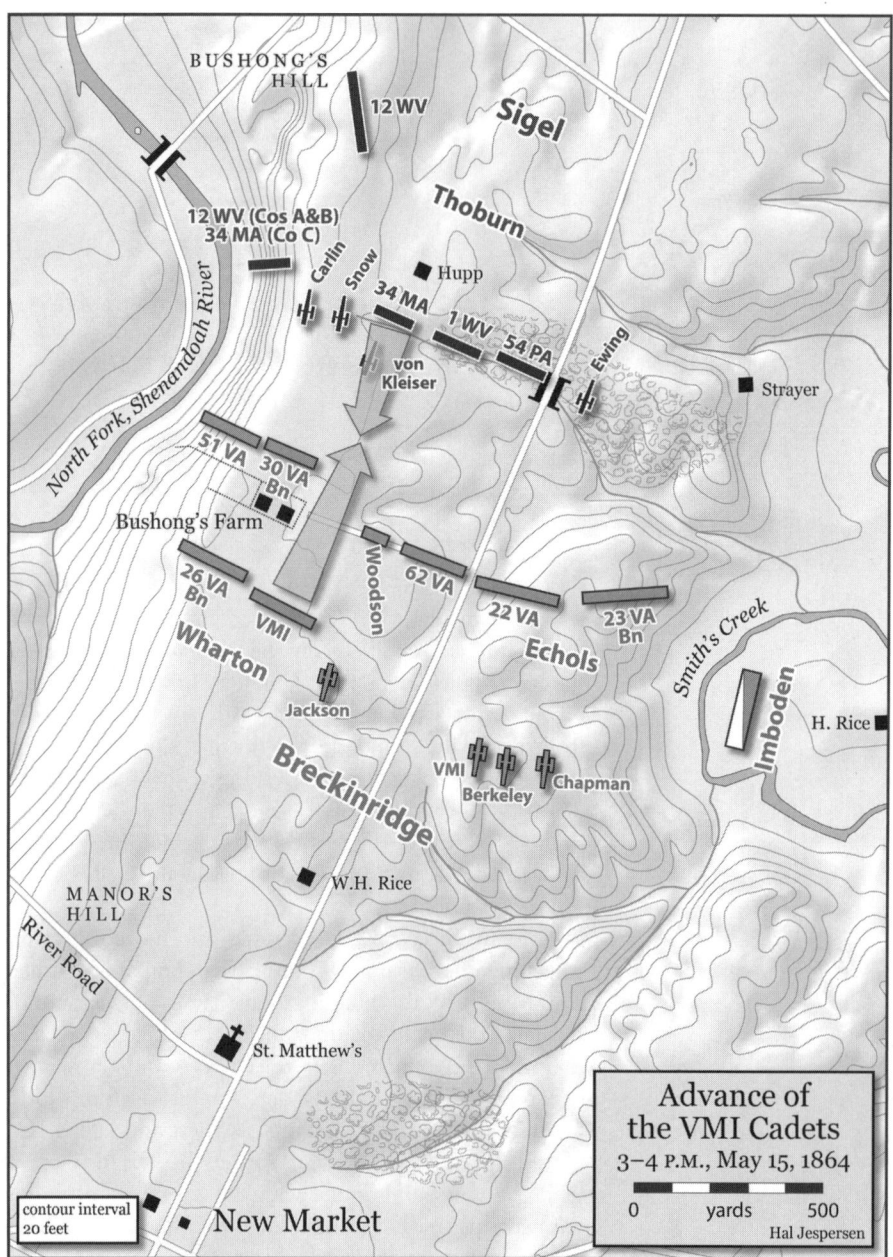

ADVANCE OF THE VMI CADETS—The Virginia Military Institute Cadets rushed to fill a gap in Breckinridge's line, just north of the Bushong house and orchard.

Frank Preston—the tactical officer who had lost his arm in a previous battle—ordered the boys within earshot to keep moving. Though their friends and classmates were falling silently or crying out in pain, they had to reach their position. There would be time to tend to the fallen later. The majority of still-standing cadets

rushed to the fence, although a few did stay behind to bind up wounds, likely saving their friends' lives.

Francis L. Smith felt dazed by the pain from a bullet that had entered his mouth, crushed his jaw, and exited through his neck, barely missing the vital blood vessels; another ball had broken the lad's collarbone. Cadet Ricketts—the only mounted soldier along the Confederate line, except the general and staff—now dismounted, hoisted Smith onto the borrowed horse, and directed him toward town to seek medical attention. Nearer the fence, Shipp went down when a piece of shell struck his arm. Cadet Moses J. Ezekiel ran to his commander "to ask if he was hurt & when he said 'no, go ahead' I left him."

In later years, Cadet John S. Wise penned what he had heard about the battle, a mix of stories and snippet happenings that occurred as the Corps of Cadets filled the gap in Breckinridge's line:

> The veterans on the right of the cadets seemed to waver. Colonel Shipp went down. For the first time, the cadets appeared irresolute. Some one cried out, 'Lie down!' and all obeyed, firing from the knee—all but Evans, the ensign, who was standing bolt upright, shouting and waving the flag. Some one exclaimed, 'Fall back, and rally on Edgar's Battalion!' Several boys moved as if

The VMI cadets ran through the Bushong Orchard and to the rail fence where they started firing at Union troops in the battle smoke. (skb)

Seventeen-year-old William H. Cabell served as first sergeant of Company D during the battle, until his death when the corps began its advance toward the Bushong orchard. William's younger brother, Robert, found his mangled body after the battle. (vmi)

During their advance to the gap in the Confederate battle line, the cadets came under artillery fire near where the Virginia Museum stands today. A bursting shell mangled and killed several cadets, including Cadets Cabell, Jones, and Crockett. (skb)

Cadet William H. McDowell had been at VMI less than a year, arriving in August 1863 from North Carolina—one of the few cadets enrolled from outside Virginia. His life and death have been popularized in a children's book called *Ghost Cadet*, which has introduced many young folks to the story of the VMI Cadets at New Market. (vmi)

to obey. Pizzini, the first sergeant, of B Company, with his Corsican blood at the boiling point, cocked his rifle and proclaimed that he would shoot the first man who ran. Preston, brave and inspiring in command of B Company, smilingly lay down upon his remaining arm with a remark that he would at least save that. Colonna, cadet captain of D, was speaking low to the men of his company words of encouragement, and bidding them shoot close. The Corps was being decimated.

Captain Henry A. Wise, a VMI graduate who had returned after a parole, took command. Cadets remembered him moving heroically along their firing line, encouraging and directing. At some point, the back seat of Wise's trousers got shot away, leaving the commander embarrassed but unscathed. Another incident imprinted in the cadets' memories of their young leader: Wise had long been noted for his piety at the Institute, but in battle, his cadets listened with astonishment to swear words that suddenly came from his mouth. Apparently, battle had brought out a hidden side of their usually calm and reserved leader, though he later denied his use of expletives.

Cadet Ezekiel fought shoulder to shoulder with Charles C. Randolph, who had been a courier for "Stonewall" Jackson before his cadetship. With battle experience already, Randolph declared to his comrade with a smile, "There's no use dodging boys, if a ball's going to hit you, it'll hit you anyway." A few minutes later, Randolph tumbled down with a bad wound in the shoulder; Ezekiel was convinced he was dead, but would later discover his buddy had survived.

Perhaps there was truth in Randolph's words. Cadet James B. Preston had a lucky escape. "I was slightly wounded but never reported it," he admitted. "I had a little Testament in my left vest pocket. A spent ball hit the Testament and I was unconscious for a short time. When I regained my consciousness I was washing my hands in a mud puddle. . . ."

Across the open field, Von Kleiser's guns pounded the boys' position as the 34th Massachusetts and 1st West Virginia fired their rifles and fought a battle all their own. They had repulsed the Confederate advance, forcing them back to their Bushong line and creating the gap the cadets now filled.

Col. Wells from the 34th reported what happened next on his portion of the Union line:

Cadet Samuel Atwill received a leg wound, but the surgeons thought he would recover. Moved to Staunton after the battle, all seemed well until he contracted "lockjaw" (tetanus) and died on July 20, 1864, after terrible suffering. (vmi)

Just then Colonel Thoburn, brigade commander, rode along the lines telling the men to "prepare to charge." He rode by me shouting some order I could not catch, and went to the regiment on my left [1st West Virginia Infantry], which immediately charged. I supposed this to be his order to me, and I commanded to fix bayonets and charge. The men fairly sprang forward. As we neared the crest of the [Bushong] hill we met the entire rebel force [probably Wharton's brigade] advancing and firing. The regiment on my left [1st West Virginia Infantry], which first met the fire, turned and went back, leaving the Thirty-fourth rushing alone into the enemy's line. I shouted to them to halt but could not make a single man hear or heed me. . . . I was able to run along the lines, and, seizing the color bearer by the shoulder, hold him fast as the only way of stopping the regiment. The wings surged ahead, but, losing sight of the colors, halted. The alignment rectified, we faced about and marched back to our position in common time. I could hear the officers saying to the men, and the men to each other, "Don't run!"—"Keep your line!"—"Common time!" &c. On reaching our position the regiment was halted, faced about, and resumed its fire. The path of the regiment between our line and the fence was sadly strewn with our fallen.

Henry A. Wise, one of the tactical officers, moved along his company lines, shouting orders to the cadets laced with profanities—a fact that shocked the boys who had often been lectured about avoiding such language by this pious officer. (vmi)

The batteries to the right of the Massachusetts and West Virginia men faced danger from Wharton's brigade, particularly the 51st Virginia. Using the natural depression and topography of the land, the Virginians had discovered they could creep close to the enemy batteries and by using the land to their advantage remain relatively hidden. The Union guns could not depress low enough to blast the companies moving upon them. Only the 75 foot cliff above the river prevented the Virginians

from making a complete flanking maneuver. Hampered by the cliffs and by the Union boys who fought back to protect the guns, the 51st advanced and fell back several times.

The guns were in the Confederates' sights. If the

Looking toward the Bushong Farm and cadets' position during the battle from Von Kleiser's guns. The 34th Massachusetts also made their charge into this field. (skb)

batteries at the crest of Bushong's Hill were captured or forced to move, the field would significantly open for another sweeping advance. Farther down the line, the cadets—opposite Von Kleiser's battery—began to get the same idea.

By this time, Sigel and Breckinridge had lost direct command of the fight that would determine their praise or censure as military commanders. Even brigade commanders—like Thoburn or Wharton—had limited control. Decisions, advances, and retreats were created on the regimental level. The smoke-filled battlefield crashed with artillery and musketry fire as the battle turned into a unit- or individual-level struggle for survival and possession.

Unfortunately for Sigel, his hungry, road-weary men were reaching a breaking point. Fighting by regiment limited their effective power and decimated the units. With the 62nd and 22nd Virginians breaking the Pennsylvanians near the pike and the western part of the Confederate line starting to obsess about the Union guns, the Federals faced potential disaster. Luck would be on the Confederate side with a concentrated, uncoordinated, and sudden forward movement that would lead to the day's final decisive moments.

Colonel George Wells, commander of the 34th Massachusetts, survived the battle of New Market, but died after the battle of Cedar Creek in October 1864. He is buried in Winchester National Cemetery. (skb)

The west part of the Confederate line extended over this ground, including the 51st Virginia, the 30th Virginia Battalion, and the 26th Virginia. The rise of Bushong Hill allowed them to creep up on the Union position and shelter from the artillery fire during their sneaky advance. If you walk up along their position, crouch low and notice how the marker cannons at the top are no longer visible. (skb)

Along the Confederate Lines

As you walk along the rail fence and look south, you can see the Virginia Museum of the Civil War. Approximately there, the shell that killed three cadets struck. The corps came across that incline, split around the Bushong House, and reunited in the orchard, rushing toward where you stand now. Along this fence, they knelt and fired into the battle smoke at any figures or fire flashes they could see.

Note the opening in the rail fence. Later, you will return to this point. For now, to continue on the extended walking tour, walk up the incline along the fence and single tree line. As you approach the trees near the river cliff, start exploring the 51st Virginia position. There are cannons sitting atop Bushong's Hill and marking some of the gun placements used by the Union. Use these cannons to help visualize when and where the Virginians would have been out of direct fire as they crept toward the line.

If you do not wish to climb the hill again after crossing the "Field of Lost Shoes" (Chapter 15), continue along the path and enjoy the views of the Shenandoah River from the overlooks. Take in the sight of the entire battlefield from the Union cannon position.

Return to the break in the fence at the cadets' position to cross the open field in their historic footsteps. Notice the single gun across the field. This marks the position of Von Kleiser's Battery.

"Take the Guns"
CHAPTER FOURTEEN
MAY 15, 1864—MID-AFTERNOON

From his position on the ground, the injured Lt. Colonel Shipp watched his cadets, unable to command them due to his wound, and unable even to make his voice heard in the battle cacophony. As the Union artillery blasted and the 34th Massachusetts and 1st West Virginia made their advances, "[t]he fire was withering. It seemed impossible that any living creature could escape; and here we sustained our heaviest loss, a great many being wounded and numbers knocked down, stunned, and temporarily disabled," Shipp reported. "Captain H.A. Wise . . . gallantly pressed onward. We had before this gotten into the front line. Our line took a position behind a line of fence. A brisk fusillade ensued; a shout, a rush, and the day was won."

Shipp's official report described the moment rather anticlimatically. Others remembered it differently. Obscured by the rain and battle smoke, the cadets likely could not see the entire battlefield. The war-weary veterans' lines had taken a pounding, and with the Union counterattacks repulsed, the officers, men, and boys began to reconsider their situation. Perhaps the best defense was offense—as the books of war in the Institute library suggested. Perhaps they realized that Von Kleiser might be preparing to move his guns.

Along the line of cadets, several company captains gave orders. Wise approached Evans, saying, "Get up from here and give the Yankees hell." Captains Robinson and Preston told those within earshot to also prepare.

Along the cadets' position at the fence, some companies lay down or knelt to fire. Their rifles had been imported from Austria by blockade runners and were a little smaller and lighter than the typical rifles carried by Civil War soldiers.
(skb)

Looking at the cadets' position along the fence from within the "Field of Lost Shoes." Notice how the ground dips toward the center, creating an area in which water pools during and after rainstorms. (skb)

The bayonets met imported rifles with a determined sound along the boys' line.

Ahead of them stretched an open field, sloping downward, then up again. At the top of the rise, Von Kleiser's gunners warily started preparing to move their five guns. Victory did not look promising for the Union with the recent infantry repulse.

Historians still debate whether anyone gave the cadets the single order to advance or whether any particular charge was even ordered. Their captains ordered them to prepare, and the young men rose from the muddy ground where they had been kneeling or lying. With fixed bayonets, they faced the field—less than three hundred yards to the guns.

Cadet John C. Howard later remembered the moment. "And now once more forward," he said. "The first thing to do was climb the fence, which impressed itself on me so indelibly as never to have been forgotten. It was an ordinary rail fence, probably about four feet high, but as I surmounted the topmost rail I felt at least ten feet up in the air and the special object of hostile aim. But in clearing this obstruction I was leaving all thought of individuality behind. What I saw and heard, the surrounding conditions in which I was to be a participant, left no room for attention to insignificant personality."

Hours before, they had been innocent boys—most with no idea of battle. Now, they knew. They knew the dangers of open fields. First, Shirley's Hill, then the incline toward the Bushong Farm. They had seen their comrades and friends fall, torn and bleeding. Human nature generally seeks safety and shelter, but honor-driven spirits and courageous souls know that success and triumph does not seek timidity. The cadets rose up, straightened their line, looked at each other, and threw themselves over the fence.

The Union infantry sent scattering shots. The cannoneers started to worry and hurry their horses. The boys ran—at first together, then breaking formation as their progress slowed. The mud was ankle deep, at least. On Bushong's Hill, Union cannon had sunk to the wheel hubs. Leaping, struggling, ploughing through the mud, the cadets pressed forward. Their training at the Institute had prepared them for this moment. From their military studies, attention to drill, bond of comradeship, and dreams of soldiery, they had anticipated this moment. Most had probably imagined a more sunlit day, less mud, and better uniforms, but nothing stopped their enthusiasm.

Step and step onward. Some boys lost their shoes in the deep mud and ran barefoot. "The color-bearer ran well to the front and, despite the incessant fire which was pouring in, the cadets sprang forward," wrote William Couper, who studied the battle during the mid-20th century. "This soul-inspiring human avalanche surged onward and upward in an irresistible, wild drive which carried them through a maelstrom of mud, overshot with flying metal, up to the very mouths of Von Kleiser's cannon, which were served until the cadets, with fixed bayonets, dashed in between them and in hand to hand conflict captured one, and some claim two, pieces." Von Klesier abandoned one gun—his second cannon loss that day—facts he would have to justify to his military superiors.

The cadets grappled with the cannoneers who remained. While Cadet Evans, the intrepid colorbearer, climbed on the cannon and forcefully waved the Virginia Military Institute standard, individual fights swirled around him. "[T]o my unspeakable joy I beheld the boys in blue running for dear life," remembered Cadet Wyndham Kemp:

and here I will say was the only time that I remember when complete discipline was not maintained. Every fellow, both among the Yankees and ourselves, went pretty

A wound took Scott Shipp out of the fight at New Market as the cadets ran through the Bushong orchard, placing command responsibilities on the tactical and cadet officers. Several cadets stopped to see if their commander was all right, but Shipp ordered them to go forward. This war-era photograph of Shipp is preserved by VMI. (vmi)

James B. Preston (no direct relation to Frank Preston) fought as a cadet at New Market. After the war, he told how a spent bullet hit a small Bible he carried in the left pocket of his vest, knocking him unconscious for a short time. (vmi)

In later years, cadets remembered the deep mud suctioning the shoes off their feet as they ran across the field. By 1864, shoes were scarce in the Confederacy and the loss undoubtedly made an impression, especially in the following days when some of the boys had to march barefoot. Some of the luckier ones returned in the post-battle hours and reclaimed their footgear. (skb)

much "on his own hook," the enemy routed, retreating in disorder, and we shooting and taking prisoners as the occasion offered. About this time I looked off to my right and saw an officer that I afterwards heard was a Colonel, or Lieutenant Colonel. . . . I think he had been trying to rally his men; at any rate, a cadet, John F. Hanna . . . ran up to capture him, but the officer was a gallant fellow and would not surrender. He drew his sabre and he and Hanna had a hand to hand fight with swords, both holding on to the bridle of the officer's horse. The officer would no doubt soon have killed Hanna, but I saw Winder Garret . . . run up to Hanna's assistance. The officer seeing Garrett coming, let go the horse and turned to run, when Garret struck him in the back with one of those villainous bayonets I have mentioned, and he fell to the ground. I have often hoped he was not much hurt, for he was certainly a brave fellow.

The cadets captured prisoners and prepared to dash farther forward, realizing the Union army had started to break and other Confederate regiments had also advanced.

To the cadets' left, the 51st Virginia had finally succeeded in gaining a footing on Bushong's Hill and sent orders to the 26th Virginia to press their attack. Wharton's brigade reached the top of the hill, forcing the artillery to retreat hastily, leaving one gun from Carlin's

Union guns on the high ground of Bushong's Hill sunk to their wheel hubs in the mud, making it difficult to properly work the artillery pieces and even harder to pull them safely off the field. Von Kleiser's artillerymen did manage to pull four pieces off the field, leaving behind just one gun for the cadets to capture when they burst through the battle haze. (skb)

battery behind. Both regiments claimed to capture Carlin's cannon, creating a memory war in later years. According to one eyewitness, "[t]he Twenty-sixth Virginia Battalion moved forward and captured the . . . pieces of enemy's artillery. . . . The colorbearer of the Twenty-sixth Virginia on the advance fell with the colors about halfway between the crest of the hill and the battery in front. His comrade, well-known to the writer seized the colors and planted them on one of the pieces captured. . . ."

Closer to the Valley turnpike, the 62nd Virginia pressed its own advance while the 22nd Virginia poured fire into the Pennsylvanians' flank. The forward and flanking movements on both sides of the Union line proved to be too much. Left to their own devices and intuition for much of the fight, the regiments started breaking.

Sigel—who, to his credit, had spent most of the battle under fire—personally withdrew from the field, and the 12th West Virginia followed him. That regiment had not taken up position on the Bushong line, remaining to the rear of the batteries on the hill, making them an unused reserve regiment. Whether Sigel ordered them to follow him off the field—perhaps intending to form a guard or line at a new defensive position—or whether they left on their own accord remains an unanswered question.

For most of the Union regiments on the field, "fighting mit Sigel" proved confusing. At the regimental level, officers and men believed they had done their best. Colonel Wells of the 34th Massachusetts praised his men, saying, "I can only say for the regiment that the coolness and gallantry of the officers filled me with admiration, and I cannot recall, without deep emotion, the cheerful endurance by the men of the extraordinary hardships

This memorial statue for Massachusetts soldiers stands in Winchester National Cemetery, honoring the sacrifices of men from the Bay State and their fights in the Shenandoah Valley. Col. Wells of the 34th Massachusetts is buried nearby. (skb)

of the march, and the spontaneous and hearty devotion with which they offered their lives to their country." The Massachusetts men displayed "a fire and heroism which cannot be excelled."

When they had time to reflect, many of the Union soldiers concluded they had fought bravely and doubted their German-American general's plans and abilities. Some even recognized that Sigel had fought piecemeal, throwing regiments into the fight rather than employing a total-force mentality.

As one soldier from the battered 54th Pennsylvania said, "we acted on the principle that he who fights and runs away may live to fight another day." Still, as they left the field, the Union boys had about three miles of muddy fields, roads, and swollen streams to cross while exultant Rebels chased them. They could only hope that the single bridge over the Shenandoah River at Mount Jackson was still intact and that someone would provide a rearguard.

At the Field of Lost Shoes

Today a gold-colored cannon memorializes the VMI Cadets' charge and cannon capture. Every year, the incoming class of cadets charges across the field and rallies at the cannon, remembering and honoring their predecessors' historic moment. (skb)

Leave the gap in the Bushong fence and walk (or run) into the open field. About halfway across, you will encounter a white post, marking the half-way point. If you wish, pause here and note that you can no longer see the single cannon that marks the position of Von Kleiser's battery, which had probably started to limber and pull out when the cadets charged across the field. Notice how low the ground is and consider how muddy this field would be after days of heavy rain on the ploughed, planted ground.

Continue to the single cannon that commemorates the gun captured by the VMI boys. Look back across the fields. It's technically a short distance, but reconsider all that occurred here militarily and in the lives of individuals.

If you wish, walk up to the highest point of Bushong's Hill and examine the gun position captured

A cadet's uniform displayed in the Virginia Museum of the Civil War. John S. Wise remembered, "Our uniforms, as the war progressed, almost ceased to be a uniform, for as the difficulty and expense of procuring cloth increased, we were permitted to wear such goods as we received from home, and in time we appeared in every shade from Melton gray to Georgia butternut." (skb)

by Wharton's men. From the top of Bushong's Hill, look northeast. You cannot see the bridge at Meem's Bottom/ Mount Jackson, but that is the direction in which the broken regiments fled.

Walk farther north into the field and notice how the north face of Bushong's Hill offers a kind of protection that would have sheltered the 12th West Virginia during the battle.

Return to the road and walk along the fence line at the eastern side of the open field. The view of the "Field of Lost Shoes" is spectacular and inspiring.

Continue back to your vehicle. The next tour points will be outside the state battlefield park, and you will not return here during this tour. Plan accordingly.

→ TO STOP 15

Exit the museum parking lot, following the exit signs and arrows. As you exit the gate, you'll be on George R. Collins Memorial Parkway (Route 305). Make a left turn at the stop sign onto W. Old Cross Road (Route 211). At the second stop light in town, turn left onto north Route 11.

"We Ran"

CHAPTER FIFTEEN

MAY 15, 1864—LATE AFTERNOON

Captain Henry A. DuPont and his battery of 5th U.S. Artillery had spent most of the day on the road or near Rude's Hill, between the battlefield and the bridge over the Shenandoah River. General Sullivan had ordered up other batteries and later headed for the fight, promising to send word to DuPont when to bring up the 5th. Time passed. "[V]ery heavy firing was heard, indicating that the engagement was in full progress, but still no orders were received and I became excessively uneasy fearing that my command would not get into action," Dupont later admitted.

Eventually, orders came, and the twenty-five-year-old captain galloped his battery up the Valley Pike. He directed his artillerymen to leave the caissons with other supplies along the road and took the cannon closer to the fight. "Pushing forward then with my six pieces," Dupont explained, "the whole Federal line was found to be retreating in the greatest disorder, save a few regiments west of the turnpike which were keeping up their formation as they fell back. On the east side of that highway, the Union forces were in total rout and making for the rear in the wildest confusion—infantry and cavalry mingled with what was left of Von Kleiser's battery which had become completely disorganized after being very badly mauled by the fire of . . . Confederate . . . rifled guns."

Among the infantry to the west that DuPont noticed, a Union hero emerged from the battle smoke. Eighteen-year-old James M. Burns fought as a sergeant in the 1st

A picturesque view from Rude's Hill, looking southwest. By the time the Confederates reached this position in the evening, the Union army had nearly finished crossing the Shenandoah River. (skb)

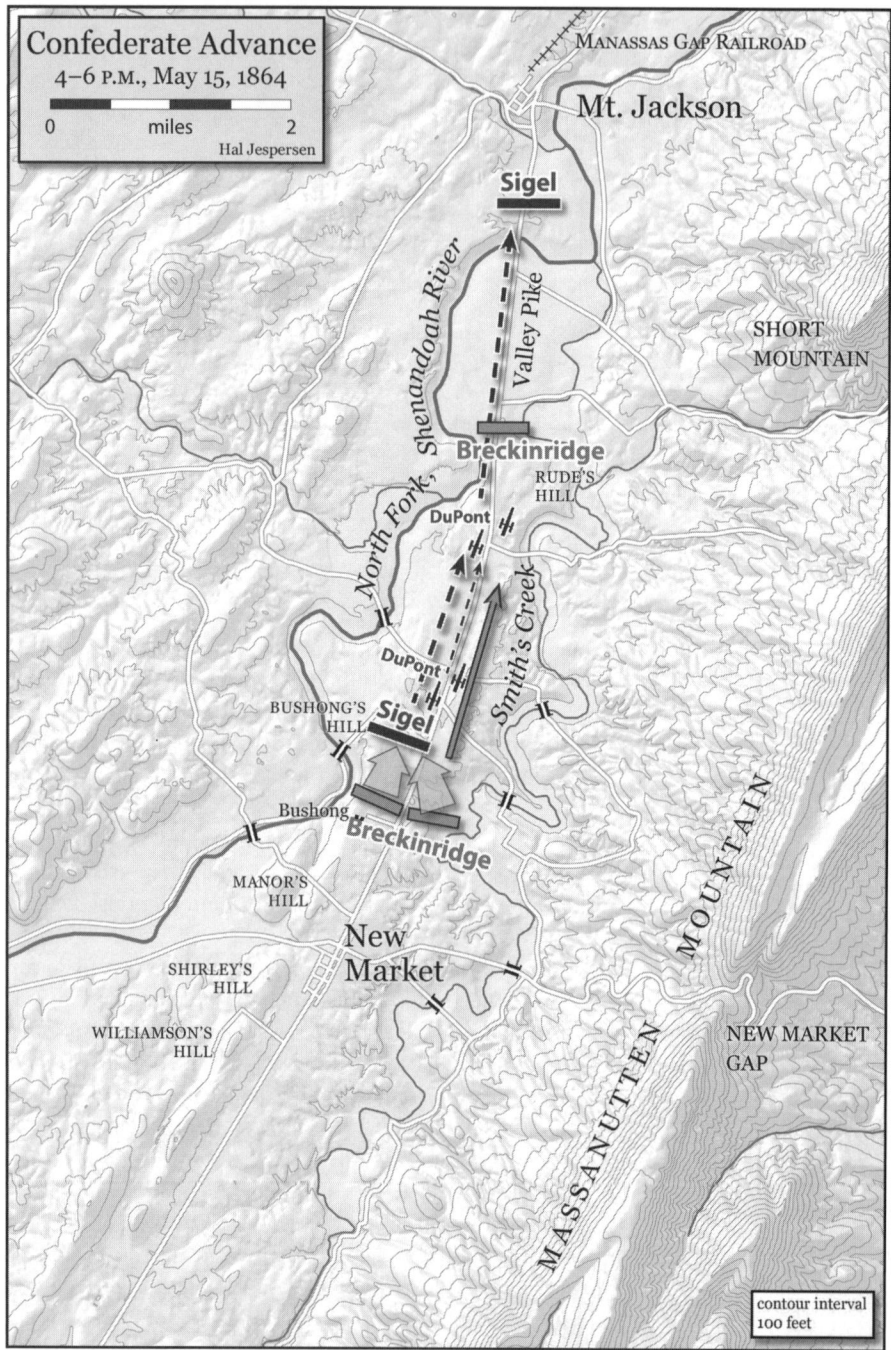

Confederate Advance
4–6 P.M., May 15, 1864

0   miles   2
Hal Jespersen

Manassas Gap Railroad

Mt. Jackson

Sigel

SHORT
MOUNTAIN

Valley Pike

North Fork, Shenandoah River

Breckinridge

RUDE'S
HILL

DuPont

Smith's Creek

DuPont

BUSHONG'S
HILL

Sigel

Bushong

Breckinridge

MANOR'S
HILL

New
Market

SHIRLEY'S
HILL

WILLIAMSON'S
HILL

MASSANUTTEN MOUNTAIN

NEW MARKET
GAP

contour interval
100 feet

Confederate Advance—In the late afternoon, the Confederate advance across the "Field of Lost Shoes" and on Bushong Hill pushed the Union lines into a hasty retreat while other Southern units followed up along the Valley Pike.

West Virginia. In the confusion, and as Confederate and Union soldiers fought in close quarters as the retreat began, the regiment's flag was almost captured. Sergeant Burns—seeing his United States flag nearly a Confederate prize—rallied several men and plunged into the fight, pulling the standard out of danger. In the rescue mission, Burns received a slight wound and one of his soldiers fell, badly wounded. Burns placed the flag safely with other Union men and rushed back into the battle to his helpless comrade, Travilla A. Russell, who later wrote, "I called for aid. [Burns,] hearing my call, returned in the face of a hot fire from the enemy and assisted me from the field of battle and saved me from capture." Cheers resounded from men in blue and gray as they witnessed Burns's heroic and selfless action.

James Madison Burns of Company B, 1st West Virginia Infantry, became the only Union soldier to receive the Medal of Honor for actions at the battle of New Market. About one hundred yards north of the Bushong House, he ran into heavy fire to save his regiment's flag and then returned to carry a wounded comrade off the battlefield. (vmi)

Years later, in 1896, Burns received the Congressional Medal of Honor for his actions at New Market. He became the only soldier to receive the honor specifically for actions at the battle.

Though the Confederates cheered Burns's bravery, they had determined to clear their enemies from the field and valley. General Breckinridge encouraged the forward movement and assessed the situation. The commander rode near the 26th Virginia, calling, "Colonel, we are mightily scattered, but we are driving them." About that time, Imboden returned from his escapade across Smith's Creek. The generals stood in the Bushong orchard, likely discussing their plans for the pursuit of Sigel's broken army.

Imboden, unable to cross Smith Creek at a northern point or ford, had not destroyed the bridge at Mount Jackson. The Federal army would escape if not followed closely. Breckinridge issued orders. Imboden and the cavalry would harass the Union's flank while the Confederate artillery rolled down the Pike supported by the infantry, which would follow up the fleeing Yankees.

The Confederate lines organized and continued the forward push, but Breckinridge decided to pull one unit out of the pursuit. The general rode to the VMI cadets and said, "Young gentlemen, I have to thank you for the result of today's operation." Others remembered him saying, "Well done Virginians! Well done, men!" He told them to fall out of the northward movement.

The young men gathered, caught their breath, and gazed at each other. Much of the day's glory had been theirs, but now they saw the price of that triumph. Friends and comrades who should have been at their

Burn's Medal of Honor is displayed at the Virginia Museum of Civil War. He received the citation and medal in 1896, a couple years before retiring from military service after a lengthy career on the western plains. (skb)

sides were missed. Cadet Robert G. Cabell realized his older brother, eighteen-year-old Cadet William H. Cabell, had disappeared. He and others started back across the fighting fields, searching for their casualties and desperate to know the fate of their beloved brothers in arms.

In the Bushong orchard, Breckinridge and Imboden met and stood in sopping mud to discuss the battlefield situation and how to pursue the running Yankees. (skb)

Meanwhile, Capt. Henry A. DuPont had been "pounced upon by a number of young and inexperienced staff officers who proceeded to give me (upon their own initiative but in the names of Generals Sigel or Stahel) the most absurd and contradictory orders with respect to putting the battery in position. . . . I then and there made up my mind to ignore the conflicting instructions and to take such measures as seemed right and proper. In brief, I was compelled to act, and did act, upon my own judgment and of course assumed all responsibility." Swinging his battery into position, DuPont's men went into action at last. "The battery was in the open and entirely without support," he said, "but a thick curtain of smoke which hung over the field prevented the Confederates from discovering this fact, and it seemed necessary to risk the loss of some of my guns in order to cover and protect the retreat of the Union troops."

Fortunately for the Federals, the Confederates stalled or became disorganized as they followed up their success on the battlefield. Some soldiers stopped to pick up discarded equipment or weapons. Others were simply exhausted or suddenly realizing they had received wounds.

DuPont took advantage of the disorganization to prepare a novel defense and rearguard action. Along the approximately four miles between the town of New Market and Rude's Hill, the Valley Pike ran over knolls and through small hollows. These hills blocked a clear view and offered artillery positions. Using the topography and innovative tactics, the young artilleryman directed his cannoneers to move the field guns in a sort of "leapfrog" maneuver. Leaving two cannon at the front, DuPont placed two more guns about five or six hundred yards behind them and the last two cannon another few hundred yards further back. When the Confederates approached too near the first position, he rushed those guns to the rear of his artillery line along the pike while crews worked the other guns. This kept the Confederates under artillery fire, slowing their advance and giving the Union boys time to reach Rude's Hill and the bridge.

If the Confederate infantry and artillery had reached Rude's Hill while the majority of Sigel's army still hurried across Meem's Bottom to the river bridge, it might have

When the Union lines broke, soldiers jogged, ran, or galloped back toward Rude's Hill and the single bridge at Mount Jackson, moving over the land in this photograph. The hill and bridge are not visible but are located in the direction of the rising peak. (skb)

been another blood bath, since there was no cover in the area and artillery could have rained projectiles on the fleeing troops. DuPont's clever tactics held off the Rebels, working especially well because the Southern cavalry, still on the far side of the creek, could not interfere.

In the end, when Breckinridge and his troops reached Rude's Hill, they saw the tail of Sigel's army crossing the still-intact bridge. The Confederate gunners fired off a few shots at the stragglers still running across Meem's Bottom, but by the time the Confederates moved into the flat ground and closer to the bridge, the chance for another decisive action that day had ended.

At the wooden bridge, DuPont and his artillerymen ordered the stragglers across and proceeded to destroy the crossing, even though they had not received orders. "As the planking was removed and then set on fire under my immediate supervision, it fell to my lot to be the last person to cross," recounted DuPont; "but no special credit was involved, as we were not under fire at the time and the enemy had wholly discontinued his pursuit." Though among one of the last to arrive at the New Market battlefield, DuPont proved his skill and talents by formulating a plan without orders to cover the Union retreat and secure the army's temporary safety with the destruction of the bridge.

Franz Sigel had lost the battle. He had tried to prepare but had failed to overcome some of the inherit weaknesses of his army. A brief message echoed over the wires around 8 p.m. "A severe battle was fought to-day at New Market between our forces and those of Echols

At Henry DuPont's Third Artillery Position, a historic event not related to the campaign is commemorated with a small monument and signs. In 1865, several local men were executed by Federal troops after trying to return stolen items. (skb)

and Imboden, under Breckinridge," Sigel reported. "Our troops were overpowered by superior numbers. I, therefore, withdrew them gradually from the battle-field, and recrossed the Shenandoah. . . ."

The Union army headed for Woodstock and then marched farther north to Cedar Creek, which they reached by the evening of May 16. Now well beyond Breckinridge's reach while the rivers ran high, Sigel sat down to report his version of the recent battle and provide an explanation. In his report, the "Yankee Dutchman" continued his declaration that it was the "enemy's numbers . . . so far superior" that "compelled our troops to . . . gradually fall back."

In addition to his official report, Sigel prepared another message for Washington, revealing the result of the battle, then claiming, "[i]n consequence of the long line and the trains which had to be guarded I could not bring more than six regiments into the fight, besides the artillery and the cavalry. . . . Five pieces of artillery had to be left on the field after being disabled or the horses shot. The retrograde movement to Strasburg was effected in perfect order, without any loss of material or men. The troops are in very good spirits, and will fight another battle if the enemy should advance against us."

However, the politic account did not assuage the pain of the wounded, and another Union defeat in the Shenandoah Valley did not fulfill Grant's plan or provide a reason for the lives sacrificed on the battlefield below New Market Gap. If he could not provide an explanation or satisfactory results, Sigel worried that his days as an army commander might be numbered.

On the Federal Retreat

Route 11 follows the route of the Old Valley Pike that the Union soldiers had marched up and would retreat quickly down. On the crests of some of these rises, Capt. DuPont and his artillerymen set up defensive fire to slow the Confederates, giving the boys in blue time to get to the river.

Continue on Route 11, noting some of the historic stops. All the signs, monuments, and markers are on the left side of the road; for safety, plan to stop on the way back to town. For now, follow the Old Valley Pike, noticing the distance and rolling topography and try to imagine what it might have been like to retreat or pursue over this terrain as an infantryman who had just been

Across from the garage and tire center, two Civil War Trails signs and an older state marker detail historic happenings at Rude's Hill. In 1862, Stonewall Jackson set up camp here, and in November 1864, Sheridan's Union cavalry pressed the Confederates to this point, forcing them into another defensive stand. (skb)

This bridge spans the Shenandoah River at Mount Jackson today in the same location as the wooden bridge that Henry DuPont burned on May 15th. As you drive across Meem's Bottom, you will see signs for a historic covered bridge; although a fascinating and beautiful structure, it was constructed after the Civil War and had no part in the campaign. (skb)

through a hard-fought battle in rain and mud. Many of the Union regiments had not had adequate rest or food, making their ordeal even more difficult.

When you see the tire shop/auto garage by itself on the right, you're on Rude's Hill and will now descend into Meem's Bottom. Continue across the flat ground until you near the bridge across the Shenandoah River. There is a small pull-off on the right, just before the bridge where it is safe to stop. This bridge is clearly not the one here during the Civil War, but a closer look at the river reveals why a bridge was necessary, especially if the river was flooded.

Return to your vehicle and cross the bridge into Mount Jackson. There is a cemetery immediately on the left after crossing—turn around there. Reset your odometer to make it easier to find the historic stops on the way back. Turn right out of the cemetery and proceed south on Route 11.

In about 2 miles, you'll reach the historic signs at the top of Rude's Hill, almost directly across from the tire shop/ garage. Pull off to the right and check out the view and signs. Rude's Hill is where Captain DuPont stopped to water his artillery horses and spent most of the battle day. Franz Sigel also stopped here on his journey to the battlefield, and General Sullivan waited here with reserve infantry units.

Continue south about 0.7 miles and pull off to the right at the Civil War Trails sign. Here was the final artillery position DuPont used before reaching Rude's Hill. All along these hills bordering the Valley Pike, he moved his cannon in the "leapfrog" pattern to keep the Confederates under delaying artillery fire. (The Civil War Trails sign and small monument highlight an 1865 post-surrender incident when four Confederates were hanged under questionable circumstances.)

Proceed south another 2 miles to the 54th Pennsylvania Monument and Civil War Trails sign. Pull off to the right. As you face the monument with your back to the road, notice the ridge to your right; this high ground runs west and up to Bushong's Hill. Look to your left: during the battle this was known as Strayer's Pasture.

If you have not already visited the monument (see Chapter 12) and Bloody Cedars, check the tour notes in that section for more historical notes.

GPS positions for locations on this stretch of the tour:

Bridge Pullout: 38.729976 N, -78.644751 W

Cemetery: 38.732945 N, -78.644473 W

Rude's Hill pullout: 38.702641 N, -78.648619 W

Artillery position pullout: 38.692766 N, -78.649927 W

Pennsylvania Monument pullout:
38.665234 N, -78.661449 W

Parking lot: 38.650816 N, -78.671104 W

⟶ **To Stop 16**

Continue south on Route 11. When you re-enter the town, make a right turn on Breckinridge Lane (where the shell-struck post is). Park in the church's parking lot. Exit your vehicle and enter the cemetery at its marked entrance gate (closest to the church) and follow the road/pathway through the burial ground.

THOMAS GARLAND JEFFERSON
ON THIS SITE MAY 18, 1864
17 YEAR OLD V.M.I. CADET T.G. JEFFERSON
GREAT-NEPHEW OF THE PRESIDENT
DIED OF THE WOUND HE RECEIVED
FIGHTING FOR THE CONFEDERACY
WITH THE CORPS OF CADETS
DURING THE BATTLE OF NEW MARKET

Where the Boys Died
CHAPTER SIXTEEN
MAY 15-18, 1864

"Somebody's darling, somebody's pride, who'll tell his Mother where her boy died?" read the lyrics of a plaintive Civil War song. There on the muddy fields near New Market at least 588 Confederate casualties lay in the rain while at least 744 Union soldiers were dead or injured or waiting under guard. The battle caused fresh casualty lists to appear in the newspapers and telegrams to arrive at the homefront with the news that "somebody's darling" had fallen. Some of those telegrams arrived at unsuspecting homes where family members had no idea their sons had been going into danger.

One of those telegraph messages read with harsh brevity: "Cadet B Stanard was killed yesterday in fight with Siegle[sp] near New Market." Jack Stanard, the boy who had longed for academic escape and battle, was dead. His friend and roommate, Cadet John Wise, had survived the slight head injury received on Shirley's Hill and had wandered the battlefield looking for his comrade, hoping to aid him if he was wounded. "I came too late," Wise lamented.

Stanard had died but a few minutes before I reached the farm house whither they had borne him. He was still warm, and his expiring words were messages of love. Poor Jack! Play-mate, room-mate, friend—farewell. Standing there my mind traveled back to the old scenes at Lexington, when we were hunting together in the "grassy hills"; to our games and sports; to our last night at the guard fire, when he told me he expected to be killed; to that

A marker in the front yard of the Clinedinst home pinpoints the nearly exact location where Cadet Thomas G. Jefferson died on May 18, 1864. The current home was built post-war, replacing the original Clinedinst house that stood closer to the street. Some of the Clinedinst/Crim family descendants still reside in New Market and continue the tradition of their family's interest and support of the VMI Cadets, which date back to the battle. Please respect the family's privacy and do not attempt to enter the yard or disturb the residents. (skb)

Cadet Moses Ezekiel (top)—the first Jewish student accepted at VMI—searched the battle area for his friend and roommate, Thomas Garland Jefferson, great-nephew of President Jefferson (above, sketched later by Ezekiel). Ezekiel found the seventeen-year-old suffering from a chest wound and had him moved to the Clinedinst House in town, hoping he would recover. Ezekiel, Evans the colorbearer, and the Clinedinst girls were with him in his final hours. (vmi)(vmi)

day one week ago when he knelt at the altar at Lexington and was confirmed. The warm tears of friendship came welling up from a heart that had learned to love him as a brother. A truer-hearted, braver, better fellow never died than Jacquelin B. Stanard. . . .

Other cadets had died immediately "on the field of honor." Robert Cabell found his older brother Cadet William H. Cabell's body badly mutilated by an artillery shell. Cadet Charles G. Crockett and Cadet Henry J. Jones had also fallen near Cabell, killed by the same projectile. Cadet William H. McDowell's corpse startled most of the living who saw it: "That little boy was lying there asleep, more fit, indeed, for the cradle than the grave. He was barely sixteen, I judge, and by no means robust for his age. . . . He had torn open his jacket and shirt, and, even in death, lay clutching them back, exposing a fair breast with its red wound."

In the following days or weeks, Cadets Joseph C. Wheelwright, Thomas G. Jefferson, Samuel F. Atwill, Luther C. Haynes, and Alva C. Hartsfield would succumb to their battlefield injuries or campaign illnesses. In all, ten cadets from the Virginia Military Institute died as a result of the battle of New Market. Approximately fifty others reported wounded while others had unreported, less-severe injuries. Dr. Robert L. Madison tended to the cadets, and some civilians took the more seriously injured into their homes. Most of the cadets spent the evening and following day helping in the hospitals or enduring a wet day in their camp near town.

Hundreds of other wounded needed aid, and for the injured in blue, the situation was particularly difficult. The Union surgeons had set up field hospitals during the battle, but the retreat created difficulties. "I established, temporarily a hospital at a little church near by, and in conjunction with some other Surgeons, did what we could for the wounded, who were hauled in to us in great numbers," Dr. Alexander Neil from the 12th West Virginia told his family.

Here I remained about half an hour with about a dozen other surgeons, dressing the wounded & doing the best we could for them, under the circumstances, when another Surgeon came dashing up, saying we must get away out of the church as speedily as possible, as the lines were changing, the rebels flanking us and would soon have us surrounded and cut off. . . . We ordered the wounded all to be taken further to the rear & dashed down through

Surgeons set up field hospitals in civilian structures during and after the battle. Unfortunately for the Yankee wounded, their doctors retreated, and the injured who could not make the journey were left behind in a Southern community that did not place care of enemy wounded high on their priority list. (skb)

the fields towards Mt. Jackson. . . . We brought away that night over two hundred wounded, all we could furnish transportation for, travelling all night and next day, arriving the next evening on Cedar Creek, some four miles above Strasburg, when we halted to operate on and dress our wounded. . . .

Whether the Union wounded made their journey hauled in ambulance wagons over rough, muddy roads or were left behind on the battlefield, exposed to the rain, neither option offered much comfort. Surgeon James V. Z. Blaney added in his official report, "about 600 killed and wounded. All dead and most of the badly wounded left in hands of enemy. One hundred and seventy-one brought back to Middletown, four miles this side of Strasburg, and will probably arrive here to-morrow. A number of wounded left at Mount Jackson, in charge of Assistant Surgeon Allen, Twelfth Pennsylvania Cavalry, with supplies. . . ."

In New Market, while the local civilians welcomed and looked after the cadets and wounded in gray, not many willingly went out of their way to help their injured enemies. Solomon and Jessie Rupert broke the rules of their local society and combed the battlefield for fallen Union men, bringing them to their home and later to an improvised field hospital in a warehouse. (See tour directions for Chapter 2 for more historical details).

The Confederate wounded who could be transported jolted up the Valley Pike to Harrisonburg, then Staunton. Some would go directly to their families while others would find beds in the larger hospitals in the towns.

Along with the wounded, other men started south

Dr. George Ross, pictured in later years, was one of the surgeons who cared for the wounded cadets during and after the battle. He had graduated from VMI in 1856 and after the war became a famous physician, practicing in Richmond and serving on the first Board of Health in Virginia. (vmi)

The Shriver family did not know their son and brother (third from the right, standing) was in battle. For many families of the cadets, the news about the fight at New Market and their loved one's role in the battle came as a shock. Even the letters written by the cadets on campaign did not reach their homes until after May 15. (vmi)

as prisoners. James Haggerty of the 18th Connecticut and thirteen of his regimental comrades made the long journey to Confederate prison, eventually arriving at Andersonville, Georgia, like most of the other prisoners taken at New Market. Of those men from Connecticut, only Haggerty survived the ordeal; starvation and disease in the infamous prison killed the rest.

For the civilians of New Market, the victorious Confederate battle in their town and fields had brought destruction, wounded who needed help, and dead who needed burial. At the Bushong House and outbuildings, both Union and Confederate wounded found shelter from the weather and medical aid. Mrs. Sager, who travelled to New Market looking for her husband, remembered the scene when she arrived at the white frame home. "All the lower rooms of the house lay strewn with wounded. Some were weeping, some were praying and some were cursing. In a nearby room the surgeons were still operating; cutting and sewing without anesthetics. The moans and screams, the prayers and the cursing were too much. . . ." In the medical chaos, Mrs. Sarah Bushong kept a list of casualties, a beginning record of the wounded and dead on the farm or in her house.

Aside from the trampled crops and casualties, the Bushongs suffered another tragedy. A message arrived from town that one of their cousins who had enlisted in the 62nd Virginia had been mortally wounded. The family members took turns sitting by his bedside until he died and was interred in St. Matthew's Lutheran Cemetery with other Confederate dead from the battle.

On May 18, 1864, another deathbed scene occurred, this one at the Clinedinst house in town. After Breckinridge had pulled the cadets out of battle, Cadet Moses Ezekiel had found his roommate, Thomas

Original burial site of six Virginia Military Institute Cadets who died as a result of the May 15, 1864 Battle of New Market.

Sergeant William Henry Cabell
Private Charles Gay Crockett
Private Henry Jenner Jones
Private William Hugh McDowell
Private Jaqueline Beverly Stanard
Private Thomas Garland Jefferson

These VMI cadets were disinterred in the Spring of 1866. Four were taken to Virginia Military Institute for reburial and two were taken to locations requested by family members.

Erected and dedicated by the Women's Memorial Society, May 15, 2008

The VMI Cadets buried their fallen comrades in St. Matthew's Cemetery with full military honors. However, in 1866 the cadets' remains were disinterred and moved to their final burial places; four were reburied at VMI and two moved to other locations requested by their families. This marker memorializes their first resting place, where they were interred by the surviving cadets. (skb)

G. Jefferson, in one of the outbuildings on the Bushong farm "lying on the floor . . . quite exhausted and wounded in the breast." In the darkness, Ezekiel walked barefoot into town, found a wagon, and hauled his hurting friend to the Clinedinst house where the ladies had agreed to prepare a bed. For the next days, Ezekiel and Cadet Evans nursed seventeen-year-old Jefferson, aided by the two Clinedinst girls, Anne and Eliza. "I always hoped to save Jefferson," Ezekiel later admitted,

and that last evening when he asked me to read from St. John "In my Father's house are many mansions" & then began to wander in mind and thought I was his mother & then his sister & finally asked me to make a light, it was only then it dawned upon me that all hope was past and in his agony—as our gallant color bearer Evans was there with me I went up to call the family of Clinedinst (who had been as kind as it was possible for people to be all through those sad days) and they came down with candles in their hands whilst I had Jefferson in my arms, and he died. I washed and prepared him for burial and carried his mother a lock of his hair after we returned to Richmond. . . .

Cadet Jefferson and the other cadets who had died at New Market were interred in St. Matthew's Cemetery before the Corps left the area, moving with Breckinridge's army to the south and east, where they eventually joined Robert E. Lee's forces along the North Anna River. New Market had been a decisive battle in the Shenandoah Valley and a death knell—or awakening—for the soldiers who fought there, but it was a minor conflict compared to the bloodbath unfolding farther east.

At the Cemetery

CONFEDERATE MONUMENT,
BARRE GRANITE.
MADE AND ERECTED AT NEW MARKET, VA., MAY 15, 1898, FOR THE WOMEN'S MEMORIAL SOCIETY
≣ COX & RICE, NEW MARKET, VA.,
GRANITE AND MARBLE CUTTERS.

An image of the Confederate Monument at New Market around 1898 when it was erected. Every year on the battle anniversary, a special memorial service is held for the fallen cadets and Confederate soldiers by citizens of the town. (vmi)

In 1867, the Women's Memorial Society of the Lost Cause was organized in New Market, a local group devoted to remembering their fallen loved ones and the Confederates who had fought in the battle on May 15, 1864. They chose the fifteenth of May as their own Memorial Day and have carefully taught and honored the story of their local heroes and ancestors. One of the ladies—Miss Martha Williamson—collected and created scrapbooks of Civil War stories and accounts. In 1898, this ladies' group completed the planning and placement of the Confederate Memorial in St. Matthew's Cemetery, dedicating it to the memory of the fallen cadets and other Confederate casualties.

Every year on the battle anniversary, a remembrance ceremony is held at the obelisk to honor the legacy of courage and sacrifice that initially inspired the founders of the memorial society.

West of the memorial is a service road—follow this south toward the cemetery exit. Here, to the left, Confederate soldiers who died during or immediately after the battle are buried. D. Bushong's grave is here, along with men from almost every Confederate regiment engaged on the field. Near these graves and under a large tree is a marker for the VMI cadets who were originally buried in this cemetery. In 1866, their bodies were disinterred and now rest either at the Virginia Military Institute or at other locations chosen by their families.

If you wish to see the Bushong family grave, walk

The Bushong family headstone stands in the graveyard of St. Matthew's Cemetery, within sight of the Confederate memorial and the graves of the soldiers who died during the battle that occurred on their property. One of the badly wounded soldiers from the 62nd Virginia was a cousin of the Bushongs. The family visited him in town, trying to care for him until his death. He is interred in St. Matthew's Cemetery with other Confederate soldiers who died during the battle. (skb)(skb)

toward the church, crossing the first road. When you reach the church structure, walk ahead and count six windows. In the row of graves perpendicular to the sixth window, you will find the Bushong family headstone.

Return to the parking lot and walk toward Congress St./Route 11. At the corner, turn right and proceed south on the sidewalk. Look for a large yellow house, street address 9349 N. Congress Street. This is the location of the Clinedinst family home where Cadet Ezekiel brought Cadet Jefferson. The Civil War era house is no longer standing; the current structure was built later in the 19th Century. In the front yard, close to the fence and under a tree, is a memorial marker to Cadet Jefferson. Please be aware that this house is private property and is not open to the public. Please view the house and memorial marker from the sidewalk and do not attempt to enter the yard.

In St. Matthew's Cemetery, which had been used as an artillery position earlier in the battle, fallen Confederate soldiers were laid to rest, along with the deceased VMI Cadets. This section of the cemetery contains their headstones and final resting places. (skb)

GPS positions for locations on this stretch of the tour:

Monument: 38.651883 N, -78.670610 W

Soldiers' burial area: 38.651284 N, -78.671143 W

Bushong grave vicinity: 38.650891 N, -78.670442 W

The Clinedinst Home, 10 N Congress St.
New Market, VA 22844: 38.649001, -78.671295

A small marker designates the location of Solomon and Jessie Rupert's home and war-era school, which was used as a hospital for Union soldiers. (skb)

"Big Little Battle"

EPILOGUE

MAY-JUNE 1864

New Market, May 15, 1864—7 P.M.

This morning, two miles above New Market, my command met the enemy, under General Sigel, advancing up the Valley, and defeated him with heavy loss. The action has just closed at Shenandoah River. Enemy fled across North Fork of the Shenandoah, burning the bridge behind him. Jno. C. Breckinridge, Major-General

This long-awaited message arrived at General Robert E. Lee's headquarters, announcing the deliverance of the Shenandoah Valley from the immediate threat of Union invasion. The results of the battle had important local implications, but as Breckinridge and Sigel sent their dispatches to their superiors, their battle had strategic implications for the larger war.

The following day, Lee wrote back to Breckinridge: "I offer you the thanks of this army for your victory over General Sigel. Press them down the Valley, and, if practicable, follow him to Maryland." Later on the afternoon of May 16, Lee revised his order with a new message, asking Breckinridge to join the Army of Northern Virginia if he could not press Sigel into Maryland.

The Confederate victor started moving his troops south in the Valley, leaving a guard. The soldiers moved to Harrisonburg, then back to Staunton where they embarked on trains to head east. The VMI Cadets went with Breckinridge's army. Along the way, the cadet

New Market wears its Civil War and patriotic history visibly on its buildings, roads, and fields. It serves as an example in miniature of the American story of battle, loss, and reunification. (skb)

David Hunter replaced Franz Sigel, commanding Union troops in the Shenandoah Valley. When he marched south in June 1864, part of his route went through Lexington, Virginia, and he burned VMI in retaliation for the cadets' role in the previous battle. (vmi)

For Union soldiers, New Market marked another defeat for their cause in the Valley. But troops—including some of the same regiments that fought on May 15—would go "marching on" until the Union occupation of the Valley was secure and complete. (skb)

battalion encountered veterans from the Second Corps who had fought with the famed Stonewall Jackson in previous years, and the cadets delighted "that they had heard of us."

While Breckinridge's troops joined the Army of Northern Virginia at North Anna and later fought at the battle of Cold Harbor in June, the cadets proceeded to Richmond and encamped at Camp Lee in the city's old fairgrounds. Richmond and Confederate government officials received the cadets with speeches and honor before assigning them as local defense troops for the city. The Institute's corps remained near the capital until June 9, when they began their journey back to Lexington to assist in the defense of the school and town.

Franz Sigel's loss as New Market, meanwhile, ended his hopes for military success. Colonel Strother confided to his journal, "We can afford to lose such a battle as New Market to get rid of such a mistake as Major General Sigel." Unfortunately for the German-American, Lincoln, Halleck, and Grant had a similar opinion, and on May 21—just six days after the battle—a new commander arrived in the Shenandoah Valley. Major General David Hunter relieved Sigel and took command of the Department of Western Virginia. Broken, Sigel declared, "It were better to have died on that battlefield than to have suffered this disgrace." The unsuccessful general believed his officers had betrayed him, leading to the battlefield disaster. Surprisingly, some of the troops who had fought "mit Sigel" at New Market stayed loyal to the general and were actually disappointed when he was relieved. The fate of Virginia Military Institute was closely tied to the next Union advance up the valley—with the new commander. Hunter marched the Union troops south again, eventually reaching Lexington—where he burned VMI—and then went on to Lynchburg in yet another chapter of military history in the Shenandoah Valley.

Where does New Market fit into 1864's war history? What is the significance of this "big little battle"? First, the battle denied the Union control of the Shenandoah Valley and an approach to the Army of Northern Virginia's flank or Richmond. Second, the New Market Campaign unraveled Grant's ambitious military plans for the spring of 1864, forcing him to revise his objectives and look for a new commander to bring the rebels in the Valley into submission. Third, the battle of New Market marked the last decisive Confederate victory in a large-scale battle in the Shenandoah Valley.

As the Civil War saga continued, New Market emerged as a turning point during the Shenandoah Valley's conflict. As the final major Confederate victory in the region, it also signaled the final disastrous Union defeat in the Valley. When Sigel's successor, David Hunter, marched through the Valley, he did not meet a turning-back defeat until the battle of Lynchburg, technically fought outside the Valley. In the autumn of 1864, Union Maj. Gen. Philip Sheridan would battle his way into the lower Valley and commence "The Burning," effectively destroying the agriculture and economy of the region to limit its output for the Confederate war effort.

On the morale scale, the Confederate victory at New Market offered a major boost. Hopes swirled that Breckinridge might fill "Stonewall" Jackson's empty boots as the next great defender of the Valley and invincible general. The arrival of the Corps of Cadets in Richmond offered a brighter day in the capital city after a string of Confederate setbacks in the Overland Campaign. In the north, New Market joined the long list of Union defeats in the Shenandoah Valley and did not improve Sigel's reputation. Grant would have to find a new general, but the defeat did not singly plunge the North into despair. 1864 was already a rough year, militarily and politically, and New Market simply added to the mood, not particularly altering Union morale one way or another.

Union soldiers passed through New Market just weeks after the battle, heading south with Gen. David Hunter. They felt disgusted by the poor treatment given to their wounded comrades by the majority of the civilians and the hasty or improper burials of their fallen on the battlefield. (skb)

Ultimately, the battle of New Market offered hope to the Confederacy and motivation to the Union to finally crush resistance in the Shenandoah Valley. Breckinridge's victory and later movements by General Jubal Early in the summer gave the region a short respite, allowing the crops and hopes to grow until Sheridan arrived.

While battles have strategic and tactical outcomes, they also offer personal awakenings, turning points, and endings. At New Market, two commanders with vastly different backgrounds battled for control of the region, but ultimately found themselves unable to maintain command as

The history at New Market continues through preservation efforts and the yearly arrival of a new class of VMI cadets to take their service oath on the field of honor. (vmi)

the battle devolved into brigade or regimental actions, hindered by the weather and fierce fighting. Soldiers in blue and gray aimed across ravines, into the battle smoke, or over flooded fields, intent on killing and bringing their own brands of courage to the fight. In the words of one participant, New Market was the "greatest battle of the war." Perhaps there is some truth to his claim. The battle has captured the imagination for decades—sometimes with historical accuracy, sometimes with popular ideals based only loosely on fact.

Certainly, the history of the Virginia Military Institute cadets at the battle of New Market dominates the historiographic narrative and popular conceptions of the fight. The cadets deserve their place in history and their shining moment of glory. However, trouble begins when stories produce claims that a handful of school boys single-handedly won the battle or records fail to acknowledge the role of other units—Union and Confederate. Perhaps a battle survivor from the 51st Virginia said it well when he proclaimed, "But give credit where credit is due. . . . Had any of the force been absent or any of them failed to do their duty, the result would have no doubt been different. The casualties all along the line proclaim the part each took in the engagement."

To give full credit to the cadets, the Union soldiers, and the Confederate troops, the entire battle must be understood. Then the accounts of courage emerge vividly from the battle and historiographical smoke. At

New Market, teens and veteran soldiers on both sides grappled with the realities of war, committing to their codes of valor, honor, and duty no matter the cost. Some rescued their battle standards. Others rose up and charged.

Pondering this history of the nation, the region, and individuals, perhaps the vision of challenge rises up, inspiring those who see it to dare. Dare to hope like Sigel, who made a new life in a new land, or like Breckinridge who overcame the odds and battled with every resource he had obtained. Dare to stand like Jessie Rupert in the muddy street of New Market, appealing to an officer in gray to take compassion on his enemies. Dare to rise up like the cadets at the fence. Dare to rush forward like Sergeant Burns when he saved the Union flag and then went back to rescue his comrade. Life offers triumph and tragedy, but those triumphant spirits who overcome their fears and rush forward find a cause worth fighting for.

The cannon at Jackson's artillery location sits silently on the battlefield today while, in the background, the Virginia Museum of the Civil War serves as a headquarters for learning, research, and continuing interpretation of the battle, the soldiers, and the civilians who were part of New Market's Civil War history. (skb)

History inspires. Its clear facts shine with inspiration and vision. When standing at the simple fence separating the orchard and field, it becomes vividly clear that in these fields near New Market, both sides' triumphant dreams died and victorious legends emerged. As the sun set on that muddy May fifteenth, the Union army ended further from its goal while the Confederates staggered, wondering what would happened next. While Lee and Grant slugged through the Overland Campaign to the east, the battle of New Market in the Shenandoah Valley put national interests, personal ambitions, the bond of brotherhood, and individual courage to the combative test, resulting in a day of broken hearts, shaky triumphs, and the reality that there would be yet another day to fight in the Valley.

The Strayer House now serves as the headquarters for the Shenandoah Valley Battlefields Foundation and a hub for preservation work in this historic area. (skb)

Eyewitnesses to History
The Battle of New Market

APPENDIX A

By Shenandoah Valley Battlefields Foundation
Adapted from a piece originally published
in the Spring 2018 issue of Shenandoah at War

When Union Gen. Ulysses S. Grant assumed command of all Union armies in March 1864, he planned a massive spring offensive that would assail the Confederacy on multiple fronts. One of those fronts was the Shenandoah Valley, where Gen. Franz Sigel commanded the Federal army preparing to move south.

Meanwhile, in Lexington, Virginia, the cadets at the Virginia Military Institute were worried that the conflict would pass them by. One of those cadets, Jacquelin Beverly (Bev) Stanard, wrote home to his mother on April 24, 1864:

> *Everybody (or Cadet at least) has . . . been thinking of leaving for the Army to join the coming battle. You need not be surprised if I am one, if they raise a company I shall join. Remember I will be 19 on the 27th of this month and ought to be ashamed of myself to be here.*

In early May, Sigel started south from Winchester. The Confederate commander in the region, Gen. John C. Breckinridge, was badly outnumbered, and forced to use any troops he could – including the cadets of VMI. Another of those cadets, John S. Wise, the son of former Virginia governor Henry Wise, remembered the day word came to the institute:

> *It was the 10th of May. . . . Hark! the drums are beating. Their throbbing bounds through every corner of the barracks. . . . It is the long roll . . . the enemy in heavy force was advancing up the Shenandoah Valley. . . . The corps was ordered to march . . . at break of day.*
>
> *. . . the air was rent with wild cheering at the thought that our hour was come at last. . . .*

On May 12, the cadets arrived in Staunton, and Bev Stanard wrote to his mother:

> *No doubt a letter written from this place will take you greatly by surprise. . . . On Tuesday night an order came from Gen. Breckinridge calling us immediately to Staunton . . . on Wednesday morning at half past 8, [we] marched 18 miles. . . . This morning we left camp under quite different circumstances, it having rained during the night and has continued to do*

so all day, the roads were awful…and we had to wade through like hogs. . . .

You must not make yourself uneasy about me. I will take care of myself. Give my love to all. . . . Your darling boy.

Confederate soldier Allmon Sager was serving with the 18th Virginia Cavalry under General John D. Imboden. Sager's son, Robert, recalled his father's experiences at New Market on the night of May 14:

Father said that after dark [General] Imboden sent out a body of infantry far out in the fields very close to the enemy camp. . . . [T]hey were so close to the Yankee camp that they could hear chickens squawking and cooking utensils rattling as the Yankees were preparing their supper.

In New Market, Union-sympathizer Jessie Rupert, the principal of the New Market Female Seminary, was among those who waited for the coming storm:

It was a night of horror, through which we slept with our garments on, ready for flight, if driven in terror from our place between the contending armies.

After midnight on May 15, the cadets received orders to resume their march, as Wise remembered:

Rolls were rattled off, the battalion was formed, and we debouched upon the pike, heading in the darkness and mud for Newmarket. Day broke gray and gloomy upon us toiling onward in the mud. We overtook Wharton's Brigade. . . . They were squatting by the roadside, cooking breakfast, as we came up. . . . They seemed as merry, nonchalant, and indifferent to the coming fight as if it were their daily occupation. A tall, round-shouldered fellow [came] among us with a pair of shears and a pack of playing cards, offering to take our names and cut off lovelocks to be sent home after we were dead; another inquired if we wanted rosewood coffins, satin-lined, with name and age on the plate. In a word, they made us ashamed of the depressing solemnity of our last six miles of marching, and renewed within our breasts the true dare-devil spirit of soldiery. . . .

Turning the point in the road, Newmarket was in full view, and the whole position was displayed. . . .

In New Market, a Union officer rode up to Jessie Rupert's front door and warned her of the coming storm:

'There will be hot work here soon,' [he told us, encouraging us to move within Federal lines.] The streets were at once deserted, and cannon balls and shells rolled and exploded in every direction . . . the air was filled with dust and smoke, and curses and shrieks.

As the cannon fire crashed down on the town, New Market resident Perry Cook was among those seeking shelter:

The shells sounded like a circular saw running through a dry plank [of wood] . . . we all went into the cellar . . . [everyone] walked the floor, rubbing their hands [and] did not speak a word.

When the battle moved north, some of the residents tried to return to their homes. Cook remembered:

We concluded to go home . . . [a shell burst nearby], and when the smoke showed us our danger, we ran back to the Soxman residence. I do not know if I opened the gate or jumped it.

As the battle grew, the VMI Cadets joined the fight. Despite orders, Wise joined the advance:

When it was clear that the battle was imminent, one thought took possession of me, and that was, if I sat on a baggage wagon while the corps of cadets was in its first, perhaps its only engagement, I should never be able to look my father in the face again.

'Boys, [I told my fellow guards, including Bev Stanard], I intend to join the command at once'. . . . All the guard followed. . . . We overtook the battalion as it deployed by the left flank from the pike. Moving at double-quick, we were in an instant in line of battle, our right resting near the turnpike. . . .

Robert Sager recorded Allmon Sager's recollection of the advance of the cadets:

[Father] admired them in their bright new uniforms and their soldierly display by holding their formation right along with the Old Regiment of the 62nd. He saw a number fall from ranks both regulars and cadets. They closed

Civilian voices tell the story of rushing to safety in lower rooms, cellars, or even a neighbor's house when battle came too close to home. (skb)

the gap and pressed on. . . . When the column opened with their muskets the hill became so completely enveloped in smoke [father] could see nothing more 'til the smoke wafted away.

Wise was one of those hit by a "terrible shell" which exploded in front of the corps:

Down the green slope we went, answering the wild cry of our comrades as their muskets rattled out in opening volleys. . . . Then came a sound more stunning than thunder. It burst directly in my face: lightning leaped, fire flashed, the earth rocked, the sky whirled round. I stumbled, my gun pitched forward, and I fell upon my knees. Sergeant Cabell looked back at me pityingly and called out, 'Close up, men!' as he passed on. I knew no more.

Wise regained his senses:

When consciousness returned, the rain was falling in torrents. I was lying upon the ground, which all about was torn and ploughed with shell, and they were still screeching in the air and bounding on the earth. Poor little Captain Hill, the tactical officer of C Company, was lying near me bathed in blood, with a frightful gash over the temple, and was gasping like a dying fish. Cadets Reed, Merritt, and another, whose name I forget, were near at hand, badly shot. The battalion was three hundred yards in advance of us, clouded in low-lying smoke and hotly engaged. They had crossed the lane which the enemy had held, and the Federal battery in the graveyard had fallen back to the high ground beyond. . . . I was bleeding from a long and ugly gash in the head. That rifled shell, bursting in our faces, had brought down five of us.

Later along the fence near the Bushong's House, the cadets filled a gap in Breckinridge's line. They were under heavy fire when:

> At that moment Henry Wise [sprang] to his feet, shouted out the command to rise up and charge, and [led] the cadet corps forward to the guns. . . . The Federal infantry began to break. . . . Before the order to limber up could be obeyed by the [Union] artillerymen, the cadets disabled the teams. . . . The boys leaped upon the guns, and the battery was theirs. Evans, the color-sergeant, stood wildly waving the cadet colors from the top of a caisson.

Robert Sager's father Allmon remembered the Union line breaking:

> The retreat of the Yankees was a run. Father said Meem's Bottoms were a solid blue mass.

After the battle, Wise returned to the battlefield

> A little above the town, in the fatal wheatfield, we came upon the dead bodies of three cadets; one wearing the chevrons of a first sergeant lay upon his face, stiff and stark, with outstretched arms. His hands had clutched and torn up great tufts of soil and grass. His lips were retracted; his teeth tightly locked; his face as hard as flint, with staring, glassy eyes. It was difficult indeed to recognize that this was all that remained of Cabell, who a few hours before had stood first in his class, second as a soldier, and the peer of any boy in the command in every trait of physical and moral manliness. A short distance removed [lay] McDowell. It was a sight to rend one's heart! That little fellow was lying there asleep, more fit indeed for a cradle than a grave; he was about my own age, not large . . . he had torn open his jacket and shirt, and even in death, lay clutching them back, exposing a fair, white breast with its red wound. We had come too late: Stanard had breathed his last but a few moments before we reached the old farmhouse where the battery had stood, now used as a hospital. His body was still warm, and his last messages had been words of love to his room-mates. Poor Jack,—playmate, room-mate, friend,—farewell! . . . The warm tears of youthful friendship came welling up to the eyes of both of us for one we had learned to love as a brother; and now, thirty-four years later, I thank God life's buffetings and the cold-heartedness of later struggles have not yet diminished the pure evidence of boyhood's friendship. A truer-hearted, braver, better fellow never lived than Jacquelin B. Stanard.

New Market residents came forward to care for the wounded, including twenty-four year old Eliza Clinedinst:

> A cold rain was falling and so many shivered with such severe chills. We helped to carry the wounded into the old Rice home. We made a fire and gave them warm drinks; but many died that night. . . .

> They told me about a poor little cadet . . . badly wounded . . . in the morning after the battle, Moses Ezekiel brought him to my home in an ambulance and carried him in. . . . Mother put him in her own bed, as it was the only bed we had downstairs. When we laid him down he looked up at me, and said: "Sister, what a good, soft bed." Mother had an old-time feather bed, and it must have felt soft to him after lying on the hard ground.

> This sweet little cadet [was] Thomas Garland Jefferson. He was about sixteen years of age, was blue-eyed, and had golden hair. I will never forget him and his sweet, boyish face. He was shot in the breast, and the bullet was cut out of his back. His sufferings were intense, but he bore up so well and never complained. Cadet Ezekiel nursed him very tenderly.

In the town, Jessie Rupert witnessed the ruin and confusion that followed the battle:

[Main Street] was crowded with weeping and excited people. There were dead and wounded men, and dead horses and broken down cannon, and many other evidences of the fearful struggle. . . . The night passed wearily away. There was no peace in its dark hours.

Union Colonel William Lincoln was wounded and captured, the highest-ranking Union prisoner of the day:

Some sixty of us found ourselves stretched in and around an old barn, near the battlefield, closely guarded by Rebel soldiers. . . . Among the wounded was Captain Graham of the 54th Pennsylvania. He had been shot directly through the right lung, and each breath he drew sent the air whistling through the wound, disturbing the dying.

The next day, May 16, Robert Sager's mother hurried to learn the fate of her husband, Allmon.

[She] mounted [a horse] and started on the long trip of 30 miles. . . . On reaching [New Market, she] was directed to the Bushong home. . . . A lady [walked] from the home towards Mother, [who said] 'I'm trying to find my husband; he is with Gen. Imboden. [The lady replied] 'I'm Mrs. Bushong. Please come in with me; I shall be so glad to help you'. . . .

The lower rooms of the home lay strewn with wounded. Some were weeping, some were praying and some were cursing. In a nearby room the surgeons were still operating; cutting and sewing without anesthetics. The moans and screams, the prayers and the cursing was too much for Mother to bear; it broke her to tears. Mrs. Bushong hastily perused the list of names of all the casualties within her care. Father was not among them. . . . "I will have a note ready for you to take to Gen. Imboden," she said. . . .

[Gen. Imboden] called his courier and ordered him [to] locate Father and tell him to report to the Bushong home immediately. The joy to meet my father, uninjured and in good health, compensated Mother for all the hard and wearisome journey to and from the Valley.

Wise wrote of the plaudits earned by the cadets:

We started on our return march up the valley, crestfallen and dejected. The joy of victory was forgotten in distress for the friends and comrades dead and maimed. . . . [But we were] greeted as heroes and victors. At Harrisonburg, Staunton, Charlottesville,—everywhere, an ovation awaited us such as we had not dreamed of. . . .

[In] Richmond, it is impossible to describe the enthusiasm with which we were received. A week after the battle of Newmarket, the cadet corps, garlanded, cheered by ten thousand throats, intoxicated with praise unstinted, wheeled proudly around the Washington monument at Richmond, to pass in review before the President of the Confederate States.

SHENANDOAH VALLEY BATTLEFIELDS FOUNDATION *partners to preserve the hallowed ground of the Valley's Civil War battlefields, to share its Civil War story with the nation, and to encourage tourism and travel to the Valley's Civil War sites.* http://www.shenandoahatwar.org/

APPENDIX B

BY LT. COL. TROY D. MARSHALL

Staunton, Va., May 10, 1864

Maj. Gen. F. H. Smith, Supt. VMI:

Sigel is moving up the Valley--was at Strasburg last night. I cannot tell you whether this is his destination. I would be glad to have your assistance at once with the cadets and the section of artillery. Bring all the forage and rations you can . . .

Yours respectfully,
John C. Breckinridge, Major General.

With these few words the Virginia Military Institute and the Battle of New Market are irrevocably linked. That spring of 1864 the stakes were higher than they had ever been and so were the expectations; not like previous years when the classroom monotony was occasionally broken up by Union cavalry in the county. But still youthful bravado reigned supreme at VMI and many saw the barracks as less than glorious. Major General Breckinridge required their battalion to bolster his understrength force of only about 5,000 men. His opponent, Major General Franz Sigel, and his seemingly limitless force of almost 9,000 men was heading south--up the Valley.

The severity of battle is no respecter of persons. By mid-afternoon the battalion could see the Union line on Bushong's Hill. General Sigel attempted to capitalize on a break in the Confederate line by moving his troops forward. His infantry attack was repulsed when the break was filled by the VMI Cadet Corps and other reserve units. Now the entire Confederate line stormed across a rain-soaked wheat field—the Field of Lost Shoes.

The Virginia Museum of the Civil War and New Market State Historic Park represents the vision of former VMI cadet George Collins. (skb)

The cadets wrestled a cannon away from Von Kleiser's Battery B, 30th NY, after a brief but decisive period of close quarter fighting. By end of the day, the battalion had suffered 47 wounded out of 257, with five dying and five more succumbing to their wounds later on.

LEFT: George Collins as a VMI Cadet. He graduated in 1911, ninth in his class. (vmi)

RIGHT: A photographic portrait of George Collins later in life. (vmi)

Collins's passion for New Market history and the story of the VMI Cadets at the battle laid the foundations for the battlefield preservation and interpretation.

For the family whose farm had been at the storm's center, the Bushongs mended fences, went back to work and eventually opened a tourist home in the 1930s called *Battlefield House* to cater to the increasing flood of visitors. Guests stayed in the old house, slept on their beds and were regaled with stories of the battle over supper in the dining room. This ensured that the battlefield and the historic house survived for another generation, but that future was unsure indeed.

On April 27, 1942, the Bushong Farm was sold to Mr. Everette H. Croxton of Washington, D.C. This historic property made famous by the battle and the VMI Cadets seventy-four years earlier would need another preservation champion, and he would come from an unlikely place.

George Randall Collins was born in 1890 in Goodwill, West Virginia, and it was his mother's wish that he would be liberally educated at VMI and perhaps at the University of Virginia. He stayed at VMI and graduated on June 21, 1911—ninth standing.

After graduation he was actively engaged in his business interests, eventually rising to Vice President and GM of the Superior Portland Cement Company of Cincinnati and Superior, Ohio.

The Great War interrupted his civilian pursuits. He eventually received a commission as a second lieutenant in the Field Artillery and was deployed overseas to France. He went into the lines at Metz with the 351st Field artillery until the Armistice about 17 days later.

With peace came new opportunities for Collins. He became the leader of no less than four companies. He was the president of: Triple Seam Land Company, Smokeless Fuel Company, Winding Gulf Collieries, and the Lomar Colliery Company. These firms proved very

successful enterprises and were the main source of his future estate.

Collins found out about the sale of the Bushong Farm in 1942 and pursued the new owners to buy it. On August 4, 1944, Collins purchased the old Bushong Farm on 120 ¼ acres and on the ninth of August he purchased an additional 9 acres.

In a letter dated August 22, 1944, to VMI's Superintendent, General C. E. Kilbourne, Collins writes, "For the last two years I have been negotiating off and on with Everette H. Croxton, of Washington, D.C, who bought the place from the Bushongs and at last (have) succeeded in purchasing it from him. I have just gotten the deeds to the place myself and feel a little pride in the ownership of the place, as you can naturally understand."

Collins had owned the Bushong Farm for scarcely over a decade before his first preservation challenge presented itself in the late 1950s. The new Interstate 81 which was started in 1959, with small stretches in Buchannon and Harrisonburg, Virginia, was beginning to grow and with it, concern for what would happen along that corridor. Since the Collins property was located north of Harrisonburg and along the projected route north, he began to meet with VMI staff about

Two overlooks on the west side of the battlefield offer amazing views of the Shenandoah River and mountains. They are wonderful places to sit and reflect on history or the importance of battlefield preservation. (skb)

One of the welcome gates to the battlefield along the entrance road, called George Collins Memorial Parkway. (skb)

how to redirect the highway so that it would do the least amount of damage to the farm and site of the future battlefield park. Thanks to his tenacity the south bound lane was moved to the east, providing a modest buffer between the tarmac and the house.

To ensure that the Bushong farm, original houses, and 171 acres of battlefield property were preserved forever, he established a trust deeding his property and estate to the Virginia Military Institute. At his death on June 27, 1964, coincidentally the centennial year of the battle of New Market, his will revealed his true intent for his property.

A memorial engraving to George Collins hangs in the entrance hall of the Virginia Museum of the Civil War, a reminder of the VMI alumnus whose vision and funding made the early battlefield preservation efforts possible. (skb)

When his will was probated it was found to contain the following: "I give devise and bequeath the remainder of my Estate to the Virginia Military Institute, Lexington, Virginia to be used as a trust to perpetuate and maintain as a Memorial of the Battle of New Market and to place improvements thereon for educational purposes. . . ."

Collins' estate of three million dollars, a large sum for the 1960s, was used to build the distinctive Virginia Museum of the Civil War and to make those educational and interpretive improvements mentioned in his will. Today his legacy continues to inspire VMI Cadets and visitors from literally around the world. The Virginia Museum of the Civil War, New Market Battlefield State Historical Park, and restored Bushong Farm tell what life was like in the Shenandoah Valley before and during the Civil War.

The Virginia Museum of the Civil War was designed with intentional symbolism. Notice how the building resembles a drum with stacked rifles. The interior displays and living history programs teach the complex history of the state in the 1860s and the details of the battle of New Market. (skb)

Today it is common for a new museum to be opened through the efforts of an august body of philanthropists. Seventy-four years ago one man with a vision named George Randall Collins embraced a unique opportunity to save the Bushong Farm and core battlefield property at New Market. His gift constituted the first major act of battlefield preservation in the Shenandoah Valley. Collins' vision and commitment continues to provide a blueprint for preservation organizations today.

TROY MARSHALL *is an alumnus of the College of William and Mary and a graduate of the University of Oklahoma. He is a veteran of the United States Coast Guard, and has worked in museums for twenty-five years at sites such as Sherwood Forest Plantation, Shirley Plantation, and Pamplin Historical Park. He currently serves as the Site Director at the Virginia Museum of the Civil War and New Market Battlefield State Historical Park, part of the Virginia Military Institute Museum System.*

Virginia Military Institute Continues the New Market Legacy

APPENDIX C

BY DAVID A. POWELL

The Virginia Military Institute's relationship with New Market did not end with the conclusion of the fighting on May 15, 1864. The cadets' performance on that rainy Friday afternoon drew admiration from friend and foe alike; so much so that over time, New Market became a defining moment for both the cadets who fought there and the Institute itself. In 1974, the 10th Superintendent, retired U.S. Army Major General Richard L. Irby (class of 1939) proclaimed that "I believe that the VMI Spirit was born on that May day in 1864 and I believe that the New Market Corps stands as a bond among all who have worn the cadet gray." In short, New Market and VMI had become inextricably intertwined.

Modern visitors to VMI in Lexington can find numerous reminders of the battle on campus. Walking into Jackson Memorial Hall, any visitor's eye is immediately drawn to the enormous mural of the battle painted by Benjamin West Clinedinst, class of 1880. Clinedinst's canvas is massive, 18 by 23 feet, portraying the corps in mid-charge. It was completed and installed in 1914. Less obvious, but just as impactful to any former military person, is the New Market battle streamer that adorns the Virginia State Flag carried by the corps during formal parades.

Not far from the doors of Jackson Hall one can find the statue, *Virginia Mourning Her Dead*, a tribute to the ten cadets who were either killed in action at New Market or died of their wounds soon after. The remains of six of those ten cadets are entombed in the base of the statue, represented by the six small headstones just behind the artwork. The artist of this work is not only another graduate—Sir Moses Ezekiel, class of 1866, but also a cadet who fought with the corps on May 15, 1864. Sir Moses bears yet another distinction; he was the first Jewish cadet.

It is worth noting that the four Civil War era cannon flanking the statue of Confederate

Virginia Mourning Her Dead, **cast in bronze by former cadet Sir Moses Ezekiel, watches over the graves of the VMI Cadets who "died on the field of honor." The statue and burial place of fallen cadets from New Market is between Jackson Memorial Hall and Preston Library. Memorial wreaths are placed here in a special ceremony every May 15 and the names of the fallen are called. (skb)**

General Thomas J. "Stonewall" Jackson are not—as is often assumed—veterans of the battle of New Market. These guns, procured in 1848, were obsolete by 1864.

Though used in drills and instruction, often directed by Stonewall personally, they remained behind at the Institute when the corps marched off to war. Instead, the cadets took with them two 3-inch ordnance rifles. The cadet cannons were seized by Federal troops who occupied and burned the Institute later that summer, and finally returned to VMI in 1875.

Bayonets are a tradition at VMI, referencing back to the fateful moment at New Market when the cadets fixed bayonets and prepared for their charge to take the Union cannon. (skb)

In addition to the several physical reminders that dot the campus, VMI's Preston Library contains a treasure trove of documentary evidence concerning the Battle of New Market. The Battle of New Market collection, found in Special Collections and Archives, contains personal accounts, letters and diaries, and other documents from both former cadets and other participants.

The oldest ongoing recognition of the New Market Cadets comes in the form of the annual New Market Parade and Ceremony, conducted every May 15. This event is an outgrowth of earlier, more informal alumni ceremonies modeled on a similar ritual first instituted by Napoleon for his troops in 1800. The ceremony includes a parade by the full corps and a symbolic "calling the roll" of the names of those ten cadets. After each name is called, a cadet from the appropriate company (A, B, C, or D) responds with the words: "Died on the field of honor." Then a rifle salute is fired, and the corps passes in review, saluting "Virginia Mourning Her Dead" on the way past. Though the exact nature of the ceremony has undergone numerous changes over the years, it has been consistently observed since 1887.

Given modern controversies over the honoring of symbols of the Confederacy, it is not surprising that the New Market Parade has met with some resistance, especially after the first five black cadets were enrolled in 1968. Though by all accounts integration succeeded very well at VMI, by the mid-1970s some African-American cadets were unhappy at having to march in a ceremony that seemed to be honoring the Confederacy. Arguably they had a point, since the ceremony at that time included two long-recognized symbols of the CSA— the band played "Dixie" during the parade, and the color guard carried the Confederate Battle Flag. A commission appointed by the Superintendent agreed that "Dixie" was not suitable, and further pointed out that the Cadet Battalion did not carry the CSA Battle Flag at New Market, but instead marched into the fight under the Virginia State Flag. Determining that the New Market Ceremony was not meant to honor the Confederacy, but rather to honor the courage and sacrifice of the Corps of Cadets in battle, both symbols were easily omitted from future proceedings.

Every year a new class of cadets takes their service oath and captures Bushong's Hill and the lone cannon. At some places, history does repeat itself—building the next generation of warriors and leaders. (vmi)

Perhaps the richest legacy of them all, however, came in 1965, when yet another graduate—George R. Collins, class of 1911—donated 177 acres of land near the town of New Market to VMI. This land included the Bushong Farm, scene of the cadets' greatest trial and greatest triumph. Advancing to fill a hole in the Confederate battle line, two companies of the cadet battalion moved around the west side of the house, and two companies split to the east, recombining in the Bushong orchard. From there, they attacked the Union final line, helping to rout the Federal defenders and capturing enemy artillery. Their courage and steadiness under fire electrified all who observed them. They suffered 57 casualties of the 257 engaged, a loss of 25%.

Collins also provided an endowment to support the development of the property, and to ensure it would become a fitting place to honor the men and boys who fought there. It opened to the public that same year. The existing Bushong House served as a temporary visitor's center for five years, while a proper museum building was designed and constructed. That structure opened in 1970. Today the park is well worth a visit, with the Bushong house restored, numerous outbuildings recreated to provide examples of a working 1864 Shenandoah Valley farm, and several monuments. The

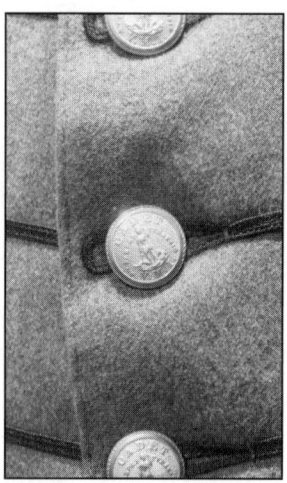

Buttons on George S. Patton's cadet uniform. Patton, of World War II fame, attended VMI and even wrote a short essay about the importance of the battle in military and institute history. (vmi, skb)

One of the side panels of the Virginia memorial, listing the cadets who fought at the battle of New Market. (skb)

DAVID A. POWELL *is a graduate of the Virginia Military Institute (1983) with a BA in history. He has published numerous articles in various magazines, more than fifteen historical simulations of different battles, and has focused much of his research and writing on the battle of Chickamauga.*

annual battle re-enactment held there every year is one of the oldest continuous Civil War reenactments in the country, drawing hundreds of participants and thousands of spectators. Among those reenactors, periodically the VMI Civil War Round Table fielded an authentically equipped cadet detachment to participate in the event.

In the early 1980s, the Institute began to explore ways to more fully develop esprit within the corps, especially with new cadets—or Rats, as they are known for the first year of their cadetship. Thus began a new annual tradition; that of taking the Rats and the Cadre (those old cadets charged with training the new cadets) to New Market every year in late August to teach the incoming class the traditions of the battle. Initially, this trip extended only one day, as the cadets were brought the 80 miles north from the Institute to the battlefield via charter buses. Rats visit the Hall of Valor—the Visitor Center and Museum—walk the grounds of the Bushong property, and form for a charge up Bushong's Hill, following in the footsteps of their namesakes all those years ago.

Today that ceremony is much more involved, and a central part of the new cadet experience. Now, some of the cadets march those 80 miles to New Market, taking the same four days' time span as did the 1864 battalion. Their route, where possible, follows the same Valley Turnpike (modern-day US Highway 11) used in 1864, as well. The march makes for an impressive sight and historic reminder, which many of the Valley's modern residents have come to enjoy and appreciate.

Once at the park, the Rats are still taught the lessons of New Market, as defined by VMI's motto: *Duty, Honor, Courage.* They tour the grounds to understand the events that unfolded there, and charge up Bushong's Hill; but the concluding ceremony now includes a formation in which the Rats are formally awarded the VMI shoulder boards they have carried with them, and which marks their admission to the corps of cadets. They are then bussed back to VMI as the newest members of the Virginia Military Institute. They still face the ratline, several months of difficult mental and physical discipline challenges, culminating in yet another physical challenge— "Breakout"—before they can refer to themselves as 4th Classmen instead of Rats, but they really begin that journey on the hallowed ground of the New Market Battlefield.

The battle has left an indelible mark on the Virginia Military Institute, and probably helped the school to survive largely unchanged into the modern era. In the mid-nineteenth century, military institutes existed in many southern (and some northern) states.

VMI's military tradition runs deep and is evidenced in the barracks, academic buildings, and statues on the campus. Here, Sir Moses Ezekiel's statue of Stonewall Jackson stands guard over one of the original cannon while the barracks rise in the background. (skb)

The schools were useful to train engineers and militia officers in states like Kentucky, Tennessee, Alabama, South Carolina, Texas, to name just a few. Some of those institutions were secondary (high) schools, and others were, like VMI, four-year colleges. Only a handful of those post-secondary schools survive today, and of those, only two (the other being the Citadel, in South Carolina) survive as places were the entire student body is part of the Corps of Cadets. VMI fully embraces its storied and colorful history, and as a result, the ties it forges among classmates—Brother Rats, in the parlance—create bonds of brotherhood second to none.

THE BATTLE OF NEW MARKET

UNION FORCES
Maj. Gen. Franz Sigel

INFANTRY DIVISION: Brig. Gen. Jeremiah C. Sullivan
First Brigade: Col. Augustus Moor
18th Connecticut Infantry Regiment • 28th Ohio Infantry Regiment
116th Ohio Infantry Regiment • 123rd Ohio Infantry Regiment

Second Brigade: Col. Joseph Thoburn
1st West Virginia Infantry Regiment • 12th West Virginia Infantry Regiment
34th Massachusetts Infantry Regiment • 54th Pennsylvania Infantry Regiment

CAVALRY DIVISION: Maj. Gen. Julius Stahel
First Brigade: Col. William B. Tibbits
1st New York (Lincoln) Cavalry Regiment • 1st New York (Veteran) Cavalry Regiment
21st New York Cavalry Regiment • 1st Maryland Cavalry Regiment, Potomac Home Brigade
14th Pennsylvania Cavalry Regiment

Second Brigade: Col. John E. Wynkoop
15th New York Cavalry Regiment • 20th Pennsylvania Cavalry Regiment • 22nd Pennsylvania
Cavalry Regiment

Artillery: Capt. Alonzo Snow
1st Maryland, Battery B: Lt. G.A.C. Gerry • 5th U.S. Artillery, Battery B: Capt. Henry A.
DuPont • 30th New York Battery: Capt. Alfred Von Kleiser • 1st West Virginia, Battery D:
Capt. John Carlin • 1st West Virginia, Battery G: Capt. Chatham T. Ewing

CONFEDERATE FORCES
Maj. Gen. John C. Breckinridge

Echol's Brigade: Brig. Gen. John Echols
22nd Virginia Infantry Regiment • 23rd Virginia Infantry Battalion
26th Virginia Infantry Battalion

Wharton's Brigade: Gabriel C. Wharton
30th Virginia Infantry Battalion • 51st Virginia Infantry Battalion

Unattached Infantry Commands
3rd Confederate Engineers, Company E
Rockingham/Augusta Reserves
Virginia Military Institute Cadet Battalion

Cavalry Brigade: Gen. John D. Imboden
18th Virginia Cavalry Regiment • 23rd Virginia Cavalry Regiment
62nd Virginia Mounted Infantry • 1st Missouri, Company A • Davis's Maryland Cavalry
2nd Maryland Battalion McNeill's Rangers • 3rd Battalion Virginia Mounted Reserves,
Company A (Chrisman's Boy Company)

Artillery: Maj. William McLaughlin
Chapman's Battery • Jackson's Battery • McClanahan's Battery
Virginia Military Institute Artillery Section

ℐuggested ℛeading
THE BATTLE OF NEW MARKET

*Valley Thunder: The Battle of New Market
and the Opening of the Shenandoah Valley Campaign, May 1864*
Charles R. Knight
Savas Beatie (2010)
ISBN: 978-1932714807

Charles Knight takes readers on an in-depth study of the battle of New Market, focusing on discovering conclusive evidence about regimental positions and unit movements during the battle. His analysis of the campaign as a whole provides valuable insight on the lesser-known details about cavalry raids and the marching columns in the weeks prior to the conflict on May 15 and includes accounts of civilians and their experiences during the battle.

The Battle of New Market
William C. Davis
Doubleday & Co., Inc. (1975)
ISBN: 978-0811705769

The first major published study on the battle of New Market in the latter half of the 20th Century, Davis's work upholds traditional military history discussion and interpretation of the campaign and fight. Focused on the military aspect of the battle with little information about civilians, it offers a concise and well-paced look at the units, commanders, and battle lines with interpretation to place the conflict into the larger range of military events occurring in the spring of 1864.

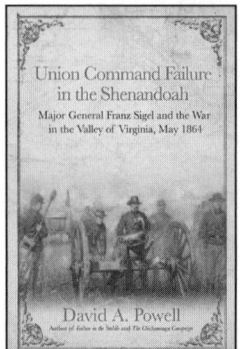

*Union Command Failure in the Shenandoah: Major General Franz Sigel
and the War in the Valley of Virginia, May 1864*
David Powell
Savas Beatie (2018)
ISBN: 978-1-61121-434-5

Looking at the New Market campaign from the perspective of military operation command, Powell takes readers on the journey of Sigel's command advantages and failures. The book provides a much-needed counterbalance to the traditional Confederate perspective on the battle of New Market. Powell offers new research, suggesting that a series of factors contributed to Sigel's failure in the Valley, rather than the traditionally accepted account of personal incompetence singlehandedly ruining the general's hopes.

Shenandoah County in the Civil War: Four Dark Years
Hal F. Sharpe
History Press (2012)
ISBN: 978-1596297609

An informative book focused on the civilian and military experiences and interactions in Shenandoah County during the Civil War. The battle was only part of the conflict that enveloped this county, and Sharpe takes readers on a journey through this regional history from the antebellum through the four years of marching soldiers, skirmishes and battles, field hospital days, and farm destruction.

The Corps Forward: Biographical Sketches of the VMI Cadets who Fought in the Battle of New Market
Col. William Couper (editor)
Mariner Publishing (2005)
ISBN: 978-0976823827

A fantastic reference book, this source contains biographical information on all the cadets who fought at New Market and their officers. Some sketches include details about the individual's experience during the battle. The information about their post-battle, post-war lives is particularly interesting and reinforces the VMI tradition of service to community, state, and nation through many different professions.

Letters of a New Market Cadet
J. B. Stanard; John Gilchrist Barrett, Robert K. Turner (editors)
University of North Carolina Press (1961)
ISBN: 978-1258165406

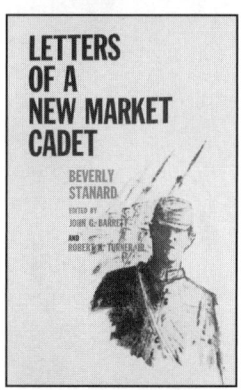

Revealing (and complaining) about life at VMI in the months prior the battle, Stanard's letters to his mother and sister are entertaining and poignant. The book includes the letter he wrote in Staunton during the march to New Market and the text of the telegrams informing his family that he had been killed in the fight.

The End of an Era
John S. Wise
(1902)
ISBN: 978-1296547295

Wise was a terrific storyteller, anxious to share his memories about the Old South and his feelings and memories about the war. Although Southern, he turned rather pro-Union in his sentiments by the end of the war but still retained his dedication to his comrades in battle. The chapters about his experiences at VMI, on the march to New Market, and his memories and collected accounts of the battle offer interesting and insightful study.

About the Author

Sarah Kay Bierle, managing editor at Emerging Civil War and conference coordinator for Gazette665, graduated from Thomas Edison State College with a BA in History and has spent the last few years exploring ways to share quality historical research in ways that will inform and inspire modern audiences.

Her interest in history began at a young age, and through the years, she has helped to prepare teaching activities and planned historical events for private school students. Recently, she has presented her research at Civil War Round Tables and historical groups in California and across the nation, including the National Museum of Civil War Medicine. *Call Out The Cadets* is Sarah's first non-fiction history book, though in previous years she has published three historical fiction books in an effort to make historical accounts and details more accessible audiences outside the history field.

Currently, Sarah is working on several Civil War research projects involving the citizens and armies in Virginia's Shenandoah Valley.